RE-DESIGNING YOUTH SPORT

Many observers have pointed out what is wrong with youth sport: an emphasis on winning at all costs; parental over-involvement; high participation costs that exclude many families; lack of vigorous physical activity; low levels of player engagement; and no focus on development. Currently, most attempts at righting the wrongs of youth sport have focused on coach education and curriculum, but in this book, the authors offer a different approach—one that involves changing the game itself.

Re-Designing Youth Sport combines vivid examples and case studies of innovative sport programs that are re-designing their sport with a comprehensive toolkit for practitioners on how to change their game for bigger and better outcomes. It offers a fresh and exciting perspective on the seemingly intractable issues in sport. It presents a practical and empowering pathway for readers to apply the examples and tools to the outcomes that they aspire to achieve in their sport, such as increased fun and excitement, life-skills building, gender inclusion, increased sportspersonship, greater parity and avoidance of one-sided competition, and positive parental roles. The book also reveals how community leagues as well as national and international sport governing bodies are using re-Design to accelerate player skill development, tactical awareness, and physical fitness.

John McCarthy, clinical faculty in Boston University's School of Education, is the founder and Director of the BU Institute for Athletic Coach Education. He works with coaches and youth sport organizations to reclaim the purpose of sport for youth development.

Lou Bergholz is the chief knowledge officer at Edgework Consulting, a Boston-based firm that is focused on developing great teams. A component of the company's work supports innovative approaches to sports-based youth development with programs around the world. Lou has helped design and implement programs across four continents, where he has focused on areas such as issues of mental health and trauma, violence reduction, HIV prevention, and gender-based violence.

Megan Bartlett is Chief Program Officer at Up2Us Sports, a national coalition of more than 1000 organizations that use sport to promote positive youth development. She oversees training, research and dissemination of evaluation tools that enable organizations to provide high quality programs for youth across the country.

RE-DESIGNING YOUTH SPORT

Change the Game

John McCarthy, Lou Bergholz, and Megan Bartlett

NEW YORK AND LONDON

First published 2016
by Routledge
711 Third Avenue, New York, NY 10017

and by Routledge
2 Park Square, Milton Park, Abingdon, Oxon, OX14 4RN

Routledge is an imprint of the Taylor & Francis Group, an informa business

© 2016 Taylor & Francis

The right of John McCarthy, Lou Bergholz, and Megan Bartlett to be identified as author of this work has been asserted by them in accordance with sections 77 and 78 of the Copyright, Designs and Patents Act 1988.

All rights reserved. No part of this book may be reprinted or reproduced or utilized in any form or by any electronic, mechanical, or other means, now known or hereafter invented, including photocopying and recording, or in any information storage or retrieval system, without permission in writing from the publishers.

Trademark notice: Product or corporate names may be trademarks or registered trademarks, and are used only for identification and explanation without intent to infringe.

Library of Congress Cataloging-in-Publication Data
A catalog record for this book has been requested

ISBN: 978-1-138-85219-8 (hbk)
ISBN: 978-1-138-85220-4 (pbk)
ISBN: 978-1-315-63939-0 (ebk)

Typeset in Bembo
by Apex CoVantage, LLC

Printed and bound in Great Britain by
TJ International Ltd, Padstow, Cornwall

CONTENTS

Preface		*vii*
Acknowledgements		*xi*
	Introduction: Changing the Game	1
1	What Is Sport System Re-Design?	11
2	The Five Domains of Sport System Re-Design	19
3	Why Change the Game . . . and Why Now?	31
4	Sources of Inspiration	45
5	Case Studies	63
6	The Sport System Re-Design Toolkit: Part One	83
7	The Sport System Re-Design Toolkit: Part Two	99
8	Conclusion	109

Appendix A: Sport System Re-Design: Historical Timelines of Popular Sports	*115*
Appendix B: Examples of Invented and Adapted Sports	*131*
Appendix C: Matrix of Sport System Re-Designs	*163*
Index	*175*

PREFACE

Changing the Game, or what we formally call Sport System Re-Design (SSRD), is the result of a unique collaboration between a university-based professor and coach, a sports-based youth development (SBYD) advocate, and a consultant and curriculum designer. What we have in common is a deep passion about the potential for positive impact in youth sport, and the fact that we have all followed uncommon paths to our current careers in SBYD.

We all grew up playing sports all the time. We played competitive sports throughout our college careers, and one of us played professionally. We are also serious students of sport, from the academic to the professional to the youth levels. We have coached. And we have worked in youth sport programs, camps, schools and many other mediums where caring adults are trying to make a significant difference in the lives of the children with whom they work.

Our collaboration around SSRD began formally in 2009. What we still find remarkable is the fact that the three of us had not met before; however, within two years of meeting we had crafted the framework around what would eventually be called Sport System Re-Design and had launched our first conference on this topic. A healthy dose of serendipity begins the story of how SSRD came about.

John played sports in high school and college and briefly at the professional level. But then his passion for sport brought him to coaching, where he coached high school and college football for 15 years. This then led him to a different career in sport: university-based teaching in a degree program for coaches, with a focus on coach development and school-based studies of positive youth development.

Megan started coaching in high school and spent many summers working as a counselor at sports camps. She went on to play soccer at Division III Wesleyan University, a place that fosters what she still believes to be an ideal balance of

viii Preface

competitive athletics and rigorous education. Years of working in a community mental health center supporting underserved families who had children with major mental illnesses led to graduate work in urban policy and child development. After graduate school she landed what she considered her dream job at a program called America SCORES—using soccer as a way to promote positive youth development for kids in underserved Boston communities who didn't have opportunities to play.

Lou has a degree in Human Development and, throughout college, had served dutifully as the reserve goalkeeper for Cornell's Big Red soccer team. Graduating in 1994, he began four years of youth-focused work and travel that took him back and forth to Israel twice, with stints in New Mexico, Maine and Ohio. He built after-school programs for new immigrants arriving in Israel from Ethiopia, worked as a health and relationships educator for middle school-age children, served as a resident advisor at a wilderness-based treatment program for adolescents, and ran the gym at a Boys and Girls Club. Lou eventually settled in Boston in the late 1990s and since then has continued to spend extensive periods of time in Africa and the Middle East working with camps and sport programs addressing issues such as HIV, gender-based violence and trauma.

In 2009, we were each at important inflection points in our work in SBYD.

Lou was spending more and more time working on curriculum, and specifically with programs and populations where the barriers to participation were tremendous. He was working with adolescents affected by complex trauma. This population faced so many obstacles to safe and productive play in sport, from the physical to the emotional to the interpersonal, that even a highly skilled coach wasn't proving enough to achieve the kinds of outcomes this population needed from their sport experience.

Megan had moved from the Boston office of America SCORES to the national office, where she supported the program teams of 15 SCORES affiliates. In every city she visited, she found the same thing. The out-of-school-time programs were just not as sophisticated as they needed to be to get the outcomes they aspired to achieve. There was so much potential for coaches to be positive role models for the youth in underserved communities, but only if the coaches could form lasting relationships with youth and manage the behavior that came along with the challenges that so many of them faced. She made it her mission to ensure that coaches in underserved areas got access to the education they needed to be more effective with youth, to really understand what it meant to use sport as a tool for positive youth development. What started as professional development for SCORES coaches became the foundation of the training program for Coach Across America, the nation's first national service coaching program that Megan helped launch after she followed Paul Caccamo from America SCORES to Up2Us Sports.

Before the three of us came together, John had been working for almost 10 years leading traditional coach education efforts with youth football (NFL's

Coaching Academy and later, USA Football coaching schools). Convinced of the societal importance of good coaching, in 2004, John started the Institute for Athletic Coach Education at Boston University's School of Education. He worked on several initiatives aimed at coach development. But despite his commitment to the importance of this work, he came to recognize the limitations of working solely with coaches or even coach educators.

We first formally came together in 2009, when Megan asked us to help train urban youth coaches through Up2Us Sports. The more we worked together and the more we shared our hopes and frustrations around the state of youth sport in America, the more we found that we had all been bumping into the same wall: traditional coach education and even high quality youth-centered curriculum didn't seem to be enough. In fact, we were coming to the conclusion that no matter how skilled you were as a coach, no matter how much you focused on youth development outcomes with the players on your team, all of your good work could be eroded in seconds by a terrible coach, referee or even a fan, who could negatively impact the entire experience of your players.

This sobering reality produced a powerful observation: every sport is inherently a *system*, with many interconnected and interdependent parts. When the parts of the system align, sport—at any level—works its magic. There is excitement, there is skill development, there is teamwork, and there are truly great games. Conversely, when the parts of the system do not align, the system crumbles, and the dark sides of sport surface. It was a critical realization for us. If we want to create the most powerful sport experience possible for youth, then we need to look at all the parts of the system. And we need to look at all the parts *together*—how they affect one another within the *sport system*.

With this systems view in mind, we began to see the world of youth sport differently. We started challenging some of our long-standing assumptions. When we met practitioners in SBYD who were getting more from their sport program than their peers, we asked different questions—deeper and more substantive questions.

We looked outside of mainstream sport and found ourselves drawn to the world of *adapted sports* to learn about some of the remarkable innovations in the sport system itself that have created access to sport for people who otherwise could never have played.

We also took second and third looks at the sports we knew and loved, and realized that our "insight" about individual sports functioning as complex *systems* was already well-known to many in the leagues and governing bodies of collegiate and professional levels of sport. And as we've researched and explored further, we've been excited to find that there are others, academics and practitioners, including the authors of Competitive Engineering (CE), who are working independently on frameworks and methodologies to influence the structure of sport in order to achieve specific youth development outcomes.

What we found when we looked at the whole of a sport, a league or even an individual competition, is that sometimes, there are people behind the scenes who are working an entire system of levers—tinkering and adjusting—in order to create the best experience possible in their sport. Behind the curtain of many sport systems, from a neighborhood program to a professional league, are people who are working to pull every lever possible to build their ideal sport system.

Once we took this closer look at various sport *systems*, we began to see the whole of sport differently. We started to see how we could get different on-the-field and off-the-field outcomes. We began to collect stories, many of which you will read about in this book, of practitioners changing their sport systems and getting remarkable results. These stories fueled our conversations, and soon we were building a framework and approach. At first, we called this approach a "league level intervention." Soon, we realized that this approach went beyond the structure of any one league, and that to be able to encompass all of the fascinating examples we were collecting, we needed to focus on the *system* view. The name Sport System Re-Design emerged as a good descriptor of what we were thinking and talking about.

As we began to share the concepts, methodology and approaches to SSRD with practitioners and leaders in youth sport, we found our audiences having the same eye-popping, synapse-firing experiences we had when we first heard the stories you will hear in this book.

Once you look through this lens inside the system of your sport, or any sport for that matter, you can never see it the same way again. We think that after you engage deeply with the ideas in SSRD, you may become a better practitioner and champion for your sport program. In the pages of this book, we think you will find practical ideas and real-life inspiration to take your work in sport to the next level.

We are truly honored and deeply excited to share with you what we have learned to date about how to use SSRD to better your sports program and to improve the quality of experience for your participants!

ACKNOWLEDGEMENTS

This book has involved many people, and we hope to justly acknowledge their efforts below. However, despite our best efforts, it is likely that there are some that we have inadvertently missed. We want to show our profound gratitude to the practitioners and administrators of youth sport programs that are working on the front lines of sports-based youth development. We have learned so much from so many remarkable people that are already doing great things through the medium of sport and games. And we are grateful to you for sharing your programs and your creativity with us. One of the great gifts in doing this work in SSRD and in writing this book is that it opens new possibilities for collaboration with these game changers in the future.

The co-authors each have some people who have put them on this road.

John: Many thanks to—

Chris Lynch for introducing me to my now trusted friends, Lou and Megan.

Georgette Enriquez, Associate Editor from Taylor and Francis, who was the first person in the publishing industry to recognize the value of our work. She took a chance on us; we thank her for her understanding, enthusiasm and deft facilitation in getting this book to press.

Dr. Mary Catherine O'Connor, who besides being a wonderful editor during the manuscript submission process, is always a deep source of support in the key moments of my adult life.

Michael Luke, my friend, teacher and colleague, who has elevated my thinking about coaching and coach education and has been a true and steadfast mentor in my life.

My wonderful and patient children—Zoey, Luke and Shayna—for putting up with me writing a book. I love them beyond words.

xii Acknowledgements

My wife, Dr. Amy Baltzell, for always supporting what she calls my "field of dreams" mentality. I want to express my deepest heartfelt appreciation for her. Without her support of my work as an academic and without her support of countless other aspects of my life, this work would have been highly unlikely.

Megan: I'm truly grateful to—

Caitlin Barrett, Jai Nanda, Holly O'Donnell, Mary McVeigh, Chris Lynch, Kate Carpenter, Aaron Dworkin, Emily Helm, David Joseph, Tracey Britton and especially my co-authors, John McCarthy and Lou Bergholz, who form my most trusted group of sports-based youth development friends and colleagues. I am inspired by what they do and who they are.

Bruce Bartlett, Ray Fullerton, Gary Esposito, Bill Gurney and all the other Newport dads who were my first, and to this day, best coaches. I learned to love sport because you made it fun and did it the right way. Erin Lane and Lauren Morse, who prove beyond a doubt that friends are the most important things gained from sports.

Paul Caccamo, who turned this idea of sports-based youth development into a movement—and brought me along for the ride. I'm constantly awed by your vision and fueled by your belief in me.

Most importantly, to my parents and brother for letting me play with the boys and for their unconditional and unyielding support as I "save the world, one soccer ball at a time." And to my husband, who is always waiting for me when I return from one of my work adventures, and who will, without question, be the very best of the new generation of dad coaches someday soon.

Lou: With deep appreciation to—

Susan Wayne, Mia DeMarco, Sean Rose and Craig Babineau, from Doc Wayne Youth Services, who created the beautiful program that is a medium for some of the most outcomes-focused and child-centered re-Designs I have ever had the pleasure of being a part of, and for inspiring SSRD in so many ways.

Lenny Silberman and Sam Bloom, who took a second chance on me way back in 1993 by hiring me as Head Specialist for "Athletics" and saying yes to my absurd proposal to run a program area called "Something New." You inadvertently fueled two summers of non-stop re-Design and helped me perfect the rules for Garbage Ball.

The staff and children of the Broadway Boys and Girls Club in Cleveland for introducing me to Mat Ball. It's remarkable how one insane version of kickball can leave such an imprint on the mind! During the years I worked there, I had countless opportunities in the gym to figure out how to make sport and games "work" given limited equipment, wide age ranges and all kinds of varied and complicated needs. It was one of my most favorite and influential "re-Design" laboratories.

Finally, to my parents, who fostered and facilitated an environment when I was growing up that made creative and unstructured play a priority; for their trust in letting us play every game imaginable in the driveway and backyard (even if it sometimes resulted in their flowers being trampled and a whole lot of scrapes and bruises); for living walking distance from a playground, a park and a Boys and Girls Club; and for their unwavering support of my non-traditional career path and professional journey.

Other key contributors we wish to thank:

To the people behind the many SSRD stories in this book:

Brian McCormick—A mentor at our first conference and the driver behind the Playmakers Basketball League, who is always willing to "rethink" how things are done, and who put his creative mindset upon basketball.

Ken Martel—An unwavering advocate from USA Hockey for the development of youth hockey, who took the time to help us understand how they have brought the game of Cross Ice Hockey to the fore of youth hockey in the U.S.

Dean Conway—For his vision of what youth soccer can and should be; for his conviction in the face of significant initial resistance; and for his humble and unassuming approach, which allows his remarkable re-Designs and impact to speak for themselves.

Rahul Brahmabatt—An eloquent storyteller and tireless champion for re-Design and a constant source of inspiration for what can be done for young people when sport is designed for intentional outcomes.

Lawrence Cann—One of the most visionary practitioners in youth sport, who has built a national organization leveraging curriculum, coach education and SSRD in a powerful and integrated way.

Mark Griffin—A leader in the sports-based youth development field, who sets the field standard for thinking intentionally about how to leverage the sport environment to make sure kids are learning.

Kirk Anderson—He was willing to share the story of how the USTA completely transformed youth tennis. If every governing body had a Director of Coaching like Kirk, youth sports would no longer have a problem.

We would also like to acknowledge the following people and organizations for their important contributions to this body of work:

- Susan Golbe, who has searched high and low for re-Designs, championed quidditch, and without whom we would not have been able to run our conferences. She is truly super.
- Eren Munir and Jessica Lipsey, for their logistics support and vital contributions at our early conferences.
- Maren Rojas, for her in-depth research about the history of sport and about invented and adapted sports.
- Diana Cutaia, who helped us launch our SSRD work as a mentor in the first conference.

xiv Acknowledgements

- The students from John's Sport Theory and Social Systems classes, especially Jake Cooper, for their willingness to think about sports in a new way and their willingness to help John make it to class (and our conferences and meetings) on time.
- The LA84 Foundation and the Booth Ferris Foundation, for sponsoring our conferences in Los Angeles and New York, respectively.
- Ethan Rimdzius, for his excellent copy-editing and careful work on our citations.

INTRODUCTION

Changing the Game

In this chapter, we present you with several examples of what we call Sport System Re-Design (SSRD). We then describe the concept more fully, and finally provide an overview of the book. Our examples here and in the rest of the book range across the globe and over centuries. But to begin, we'll start locally. Let's look at an example of how one committed individual changed the game for parents, kids and others. We'll consider both his *reasons* for bringing about a change and his *methods* in carrying out the change.

JP Youth Soccer: A Local Example

Dean Conway played lots of sports as a kid growing up in Massachusetts, including baseball, basketball, pond hockey and soccer. He loved the excitement of competition. Soccer became a central focus for him as he got older, and he has seen a lot of it, in different places. He has a United States Soccer Federation "A" level coaching license, and has coached at the high school, college and professional levels. But because he loves the pure enjoyment of the game, he came to focus on kids playing soccer.

When Dean was asked to become the director of Massachusetts Youth Soccer, one of the largest youth sport organizations in the United States, he signed on. But over time, he became dissatisfied. One thing became crystal clear: he did not like what happened on game day.

When you hear Dean speak about it, he sounds a bit like a beat poet. Trying to put it to words he says, "The vibe surrounding the kids on the day of the game is off. The parents are often a bit too intense, and the coaches just don't get it." What "it" is for Dean is the experience of the joy of competition without the

2 Introduction

adult angst intervening. The coaches are not able to help kids experience the joy of competition because they don't know how to deal with the parental tension that is all too common in such settings. He also found that frequent blowouts—lopsided games—inhibited many kids from really benefitting from all that game day has to offer.

Dean and a few of his close associates got together and started their own league in his neighborhood in Boston: Jamaica Plain Youth Soccer (JPYS). As a student of the game, Dean had studied how soccer was played around the world. He admired the creative flair with which players on many of the teams from the African continent played. He admired the control and team play of the Dutch. What he saw in his home state, however, did not resemble that in any way.

So Dean and his colleagues at JPYS tinkered with some elements of the game day to try to bring about a different result. One of the things that seemed to interfere with the games was the adult coaches making decisions about who should play, and what role they could play. In his view, this prevented lots of kids from experiencing the range of skills and situations that go into learning to play soccer.

Another factor that interfered with the game involved parents. Parents would plant themselves in folding chairs uncomfortably close to the boundaries of the playing field and would try to coach the players while complaining about the referees or complaining about the coaches or even complaining about other parents. These issues seemed to worsen during blowout games.

So Dean and JPYS did away with teams in their Under 10 league. Now this might sound nonsensical: how do you play games without teams? And why would this help with the other problems? First, Dean put the parents to work: not as coaches, but setting up the field and composing teams. When eight kids showed up and signed in, they were composed into two teams by parents. Result: no more waiting around for the last kid or officials or coaches to show up. Once you have eight kids, they head to the nearest marked field and get playing! It turns out that this change resulted in other positive changes, both with interfering parents and with blowouts.

These small-sided (4v4) games were played on a small field with small goals and no goalkeepers. Players seemed more carefree and appeared less anxious. They had more control over the decision-making. Adults were more relaxed and objective—they didn't yell advice at the kids; they clapped for good plays. They were more patient and seemed to understand that it was all about developing skills!

This change also helped them address the issue of blowouts. Staff would monitor how the games were proceeding. If the sides seemed uneven, someone from the league would make a quick adjustment of the team (change reversible jerseys with a few kids) and off they would go, playing a game with a bit more parity. The second way they re-engineered the game was to play games to three goals. In a game where three goals wins, it is harder for the players to get that feeling of despair that comes before a blowout. They are always within reach of potentially winning the game.

But we *can't* change real games . . . can we? Some readers might appreciate the example above, yet consider it to be just an interesting "one-off" example of local variation. Many would still be taken aback by the thought of changing a revered "real" game. Youth soccer for kids under 10 is one thing. And yes, it's true, baseball has been changed for very young children by using a tee for the ball. But "tee-ball" is not the same as real baseball. You wouldn't make changes like this to the game for older kids, and certainly not for adults. We definitely can't tamper with the big three: football, baseball and basketball. Can we?

Basketball: A Historical Example

Imagine you're a physical education teacher and you have a rowdy bunch of boys who are getting tired of being confined indoors during the long New England winter. Then your short-tempered boss, the principal, strides into your class to let you know that he does not like the way things look. He proceeds to insist that you come up with an "athletic distraction that does not take up too much room, that could help to keep the students in shape" for their spring sport, track. He explicitly emphasizes to "make it fair for all players and not too rough!" You have two weeks. Go!

This is essentially the scenario that confronted Dr. James Naismith, the inventor of the sport of basketball, in 1891 as he worked at the YMCA school in Springfield, MA. Given this ultimatum, Naismith started tinkering with what he knew. In his youth, he had played a game called "ducks on the pond" that required players to throw stones at a target to knock a rock off a post. He also utilized some old soccer balls from the equipment closet in the YMCA and asked the custodian to nail some boxes up on the wall at each end of a room. The custodian instead grabbed a few peach baskets that were lying around. Throwing soccer balls into peach baskets worked okay, but each time someone sank the ball into a basket, someone had to retrieve the ball by going up a ladder.

Initially, Naismith experimented with as many as *fifty* players on a team! He later settled upon nine. It was not until six years later that the numbers of players to a side got narrowed down to what we now consider a sacred standard of basketball: five. And it was not until ten years later that they started to cut the bottoms out of the peach baskets.

If you look at Naismith's dilemma, there are a few interesting things about his situation. First, he had a *sense of urgency*. He had to come up with something in two weeks to please his demanding superior. The necessity of meeting this time demand forced him to be quite resourceful and forced him to experiment on the spot. Second, luckily for Naismith, he was given some clear and specific goals to achieve—what we call *outcomes* in Sport System Re-Design. We all know it is easier to hit a target if we aim to hit a specific spot on that target.

4 Introduction

Third, creativity and innovation are often fueled when people are able to think outside the confines of the territory in which they have lots of experience. It might have been an accident that the custodian brought the peach baskets instead of the boxes Naismith requested. But young Naismith was able to literally think "outside the box" and see that the hoop-shaped basket was something that could be incorporated into his new game. Like Dean Conway in the JPYS story, Naismith was pushed to find a solution based partially on what he knew, while also venturing into unknown territory.

Later Changes to Increase Excitement

The game of basketball has changed in many ways since the time of Naismith. A few changes are worth mentioning because they were really quite radical, though now we take them for granted. The pace of the game was a persistent problem and an important impetus of change. Ten years after Naismith invented the game, they would cut the bottom out of the baskets and start making them out of wire. That really sped up the pace of the game! But then as the ball came through the basket, players would fight for possession. It was not until 1937 that players used a "jump ball" at center court to establish possession after a basket.

Nevertheless, even with these changes, the pace of the game was still quite slow and large players were advantaged by this set of rules. Sam Berry, then coach at the University of Southern California, persuaded the NCAA to award the defensive team possession of the ball after a basket. This rule change helped the continuity of the game, but games were still often slow, because of stalling tactics employed by many teams. Players often clustered around the basket, passing the ball in an attempt to keep it away from those defending them. Minutes went by, aimless and even boring minutes. This also resulted in many games being low-scoring affairs. In fact, in 1950 the Fort Wayne Pistons and the Minneapolis Lakers played a game that ended 19–18—the lowest-scoring game in NBA history. Finally, in 1954, the NBA took matters into their own hands and introduced the "shot clock"—a buzzer that went off after a team had had possession of the ball under the basket for 24 seconds.

These changes improved the pace. But still, professional basketball was suffering from a kind of constipation. Players were getting taller, and these tall players would crowd each other at the basket, elbowing and pushing to make a shot. Many exciting moments would deteriorate into traffic jams at the basket. Shorter players, however talented, had little chance, because all the action took place at the basket—ten feet above the floor.

In 1968, to make the game more appealing to the fans, officials of the American Basketball Association took another stab at changing the game—they implemented the "three point shot rule"—balls successfully shot from beyond a zone called the 3-point line would be worth three points, not two. The higher value of these baskets would be a motivation to good shooters to take shots from far outside the key.

What came out of this simple change? It placed a premium on long-range shooting. As a result, it unclogged the key. It distributed players further from the basket, creating more opportunities for driving and cutting to the basket. Audiences benefitted from this more open game. Players benefitted, as talented shooters, who would formerly have been judged too short to compete successfully, now had increased strategic value.

We take this small but critical change for granted now. But it was only one of a number of small but crucial changes that gave us the game of basketball we know today.

Who Can "Change the Game"?

Now we've seen several examples, from completely different parts of the sport universe, of Sport System Re-Design—games being changed to achieve certain outcomes. And Dean Conway and Dr. Naismith are not the only ones. Our professional sports leagues constantly change rules that govern the way the game is played and the way the league is set up. They might make modifications to make the game more exciting for the audience or include a broader range of participation. Given the constant tweaking at the professional level, why should it be that our youth sports leagues tend to be much more static? Especially considering that at that level, the needs are much greater. And in youth sport, the importance of maximizing the potential of sport is much greater because our young people are the potential beneficiaries.

Sometimes it's tough to see what's right in front of us. Some modern-day basketball players might laugh when they learn that in 1901, when the first set of official rules for women's basketball was created, the game was virtually unrecognizable. The court consisted of three different zones with three players from each team in each zone. Players were not allowed to move or dribble between the zones! Players could only move when the ball was in the air, and no talking was allowed! Now imagine 100 years from now. What current versions of sports, professional or amateur, may appear just as ludicrous?

But there is hope. There are some people who, like Dean, don't like what they are seeing in youth sports. And they are thinking, creatively and intentionally, about how to create a different kind of environment. Here is another example of a game-changer, again in basketball—but this time not the NBA. Rather, this example describes a set of game changes in middle school boys' basketball.

Optimizing Youth Basketball

As he watched the end of a middle school boys' basketball game, Brian McCormick saw something he did not like, and not for the first time. The coaches of the game were both normally well-meaning guys, but the intensity of their coaching just didn't match the stakes of the game, and it was missing the point of developing skillful players. Brian had been running basketball leagues

6 Introduction

for quite a while. He had seen this so often before, but these two coaches made him realize that he had to do something about it.

Brian had been setting up basketball leagues and tournaments for a long time. His involvement in the sport was making it abundantly clear: one of the biggest obstacles to kids' development could be their coach. In most cases, coaches could organize the drills and even teach skills quite competently—that was not the problem. The problem was that coaches would do a nice job of preparing their players leading up to games, but would become different creatures during the actual game. Some of these adults would yell at players, cajole and intimidate the refs, shout at each other and otherwise exhibit poor comportment as coaches. When the game was on the line, the coaches would change: they would care more about winning the game than the development of the players. He found it ironic that the people that were charged with ensuring the development of the players were actually impeding it!

Brian is not just concerned with how the *best* players develop, he wants to help *all* his players to reach their potential. He has written several books on coaching and developing players. Even more than that, Brian is curious as to *how to best structure the experience so players can develop.* He is one of those rare individuals who both writes about coaching and player development and also is involved in coaching at the same time. So he asked himself, "How do I turn the focus of a game, the time when players really get to hone their skills, away from the coach's ego and back to the player's development where it belongs?"

But the coaches' focus on winning was not the only problem. A second thing began to bother Brian at basketball tournaments. Not only was there something awry with the coaching, but at the end of each tournament, he found himself handing the money collected for these tournaments over to the referees. While he understood the importance of having someone in charge of making sure that the games did not get out of hand, he did not like having to pay someone $50 to ref a game of 9 and 10 year olds. Usually, the ref would basically call a few traveling violations and three or four disputable out-of-bounds calls and a few obvious shooting fouls. It bothered him because he felt the people he *really* needed to invest in were the coaches in his league, not the refs! The refs would walk away from the tournament, and he—and the players—might not see them again. But the coaches were there for the long haul. So he started to consider how he could pay the referees less and the coaches more.

And truth be told, Brian had a third thing bothering him: the format of the game. The traditional 5 vs. 5 format struck Brian as less than optimal for the young kids in his league. Brian had been thinking a lot about how to help players become good decision makers. He realized that the best way was to give them the chance to actually make decisions. One of the obvious downsides of the 5 vs. 5 format for young kids is that only a few kids—usually the most advanced ones at that moment—typically dominate the game, have the ball in their hands the most and as a result, make most of the decisions.

Brian had begun considering moving to a 3 vs. 3 format for a while. He knew that in soccer, they had been using "small-sided" games for some time to teach certain tactical concepts of distributing space and passing. In a 3 vs. 3 format, it is much more likely that everyone will touch the ball and have more chances to make decisions. In Brian's mind, more "touches" is a goal that is consonant with *all* players developing their technical basketball skills and their decision-making skills.

Three Problems, Three Changes

So Brian had three things he wanted to address: coaches not prioritizing their players' growth, giving all the money to the refs instead of the coaches and the shortcomings of the 5 vs. 5 format for kids in his league. Something had to give. A lot of people would simply stew and lament the problems. But like Dean Conway, Brian decided to *change the game*. His changes were small, but radical.

First, Brian decided to try using the "small-sided games" idea from soccer and shrink the game to 3 vs. 3, *at only one basket*, so kids could get more touches. Additionally, the coach would actually not be in charge of one team anymore. Instead, he or she would "coach a basket." That would mean that he or she would coach *both* teams playing 3 vs. 3 at a basket. *Voila*—The coach's ego now would be channeled towards both of the teams in the game playing a great game. All the kids would get the best of his or her coaching!

The third change, a more practical one, was eliminating the necessity of the referee by handing that role over to the kids and the coach. In pickup basketball, players can usually easily decide out-of-bounds calls or fouls without incident, so Brian reasoned that they could do it here as well. Occasionally, however, in the heat of the game it can be tough to resolve a difference of opinion. This job Brian now assigned to the "coach of the basket." If the players could not amicably settle a dispute about a call, the coach now had the authority to end the dispute and be the final arbiter of the situation.

Building on the Changes

Brian continued to fine-tune his league to deliver the best possible benefits of the game. After he made the changes above, Brian saw the opportunity to solve another problem—equitable playing time. If everyone is going to develop, he thought, then they need equal time in a game to do so. What he understood too well was that, left in the hands of the coach, game situations invariably arise where a coach will keep his best, most capable players in the game a bit longer than his younger or less-developed players.

While this is a perfectly understandable response in a culture that values winning, it can do real harm to the confidence of a child kept out of a contest,

8 Introduction

because the coach appears not to believe in that child's abilities. Some children quickly come to realize that their coach's actions and words convey to them—explicitly and implicitly—what the coach thinks of their developing abilities. When children who are most vulnerable to dropping out of sport learn that someone in a position of authority does not think highly of their abilities, they are that much closer to leaving the sport.

What we have described here is the classic youth sport "substitution dilemma." It is an ethical dilemma in the truest sense because it has to do with the coach making an inescapable choice that intentionally affects others. This is a challenge that coaches face and often do not handle equitably. Commonly, the league structures and administrators at the youth level do not offer enough guidance to inexperienced coaches, who might be trying to do the right things but instead succumb to other pressures, like the pressure to win a game.

Brian addressed the "substitution dilemma" ingeniously. He set up a rule that each team is composed of four players. The fourth player substitutes every two possessions of the ball. Again, this subtle change obviates one of the most problematic situations every youth coach is faced with. In Brian's new 3 vs. 3 game with a fourth player on each team, the substitution dilemma is resolved.

Tinkering with the format, Brian McCormick has literally changed the structure of the game and the roles each person plays in it. This happened because Brian was intentional about what he wanted to achieve in his league. It happened because he took a very creative approach to problems that had plagued his leagues for years. This is an exquisite example of changing the game to get an outcome; what we call Sport System Re-Design (SSRD).

Some might say that Brian McCormick is a very unusual person—more creative and bold than most. But we'll argue in this book that any of us can "change the game" by making small but thoughtful changes to achieve the goals we seek for our league or program. In the pages that follow, we will give many more examples to spur creativity. We will also work through the steps of Sport System Re-Design, to become a game-changer like Dean and Brian. We will provide specific steps and exercises to help you think through your own sport system challenges, and ways those could be addressed through a logical and clear process.

Changing the Game: *Sport System Re-Design*

Improving the quality of the sport experience for the participant has typically been accomplished through two main approaches: *coach education* and use of *curriculum* (activities and materials). However, in our observation and work with a wide range of youth sports programs, we have found an exciting third approach. We have termed it *Sport System Re-Design* (SSRD).

In many ways, SSRD is not a new concept. There is not a sport that exists that has not gone through some type of re-design since its inception, as we discussed

Introduction **9**

above. Furthermore, elements of SSRD have been central parts of the physical education, adaptive physical education and the sport pedagogy scenes for many decades.

In its most basic form, SSRD involves looking at the core elements of the actual sport experience and purposefully altering some element of that experience in order to get a specific desired outcome. While SSRD may work in concert with a curriculum, and certainly would utilize a level of coach training, it is distinct in its methodology. Simply stated, SSRD is the creative and intentional tinkering with one or more parts of the game or sport system to positively impact the outcomes for youth and other participants.

It is exciting for us to know that there are programs, leagues, practitioners and academics who are actively thinking about changing a sport system, specifically to achieve youth development outcomes through sport. We believe we are at the beginning of something important and far-reaching. It's been validating and invigorating to meet people who are doing work in this area. Some are pure frontline practitioners, such as Street Soccer USA and Magic Bus. Others are major governing bodies of sport, such as the International Rugby Board/World Rugby and USA Hockey. And others are researchers and academics, such as the team of Burton, Gillham and Hammermeister (2011). They have been developing and researching a methodology called Competitive Engineering, which parallels our work in Sport System Re-Design. Their work is particularly important, we think, because of their focus on assessing outcomes. The idea and approach of re-Design becomes more legitimized in the eyes of more people when there are more people writing, researching and talking about it in rigorous ways.

To the many people working on re-Design in their own ways, we hope to be able to use this book as a platform to rally interested parties together. We are at the beginning of something that is becoming a community of practice (Lave & Wenger, 1991), a group of people who share an interest or passion or goal, and who jointly take part in activities around that interest. For some, it may become a legitimate area of research and study. For others, it will be a productive approach to solving problems in their work. It may even spread globally as a movement to advance youth development in sport.

This Book

This volume consists of eight chapters and a substantive appendix. The first five chapters give an overview of the entire process of Sport System Re-Design, including many examples, both U.S.-based and international. Some are in youth sport; others are re-Designs of professional sport. While we assume that most readers of this book are involved in youth sport, the professional examples provide evidence that these issues emerge in all organized sport.

Chapter 1 paints the picture of how widespread the opportunity is to change the game—how diverse the issues are that sport organizations face. It provides an

10 Introduction

overview of how the method works. Chapter 2 will introduce the five domains of Sport System Re-Design, prompting you to begin to think about your own situation. Chapter 3 asks the question, "Why change the game, and why now?" It reviews some of the persistent problems in sport today—factors that affect most, if not all, youth sport leagues and settings, and even some factors affecting professional sport. Chapter 4 provides a deeper view of the approach, introducing some of the historical predecessors and inspirations for our approach. Chapter 5 provides seven great examples from across the globe and from a variety of sport settings and systems. These examples may help you see your own situation—your own sport system—in a new light.

Chapters 6 and 7 introduce you to the details of the process: they are your toolkit, and they will help you think concretely about the challenges of your own sport setting. In Chapter 6, you will learn how to prepare yourself and your team to enter into the process of re-Design, and you will work through steps 1 and 2 of the process of re-Design. In Chapter 7, you will work through the remaining three steps, completing the process. The chapters include a discussion of how to "change the minds" of those around you, so that they too can see the benefits of re-designing the sport system.

Finally, after the Conclusion, we provide some of the context in the Appendix. First is a "history of sport timeline"—this will give you a sense of how various sports have changed and evolved over time, and will provide a context to your own attempts to help your sport system "evolve." Next is a matrix of Sport System Re-Designs organized according to the desired outcomes that designers were aiming for. Finally, we include a section on examples from "invented" and "adapted" sports—these are cases that exemplify re-Design at its most creative.

References

Burton, D., Gillham, A. D., & Hammermeister, J. (2011). Competitive engineering: Structural climate modifications to enhance youth athletes' competitive experience. *Physical Education, Health and Recreation Faculty Publications.* Paper 1. http://dc.ewu. edu/pehr_fac/1.

Burton, D., O'Connell, K., Gillham, A. D., & Hammermeister, J. (2011). More cheers and fewer tears: Examining the impact of competitive engineering on scoring and attrition in youth flag football. *International Journal of Sports Science and Coaching, 6*(2), 219–228.

Lave, J., & Wenger, E. (1991). *Situated learning: Legitimate peripheral participation.* New York: Cambridge University Press.

1

WHAT IS SPORT SYSTEM RE-DESIGN?

Lacrosse is a sport that is difficult for most to pick up quickly. In order to even get in a lacrosse game, you have to be able to keep the ball in the pocket of your stick or to scoop it off the ground, which is not an easy skill to master, especially if someone is defending you. MetroLacrosse is an organization that brings the sport of lacrosse to kids in Boston's underserved neighborhoods. If MetroLacrosse wants to get kids excited about playing lacrosse, they have to help them learn this skill quickly so that the kids will experience some success and be motivated to continue to play the sport.

The Struggle to Achieve Positive Outcomes

It's not surprising, then, that when Megan started working with MetroLacrosse a few years ago, their coach training focused heavily on providing coaches with tools and techniques to help kids master this and other skills that are key to game success. Nor is it surprising that the MetroLacrosse curriculum has many activities that give kids the chance to practice these skills. Unfortunately, no matter how many iterations of curriculum they designed and hours of coach training their coaches participate in, they continue to encounter the same challenge: some of the teams see great improvements, and some of them just don't progress at the same rate.

Improving stick skills is a challenge that novice lacrosse players, whether in underserved communities or not, face all the time. We know that kids can develop this skill through repetition of the right drills and good instruction from a coach. But even this straightforward sports-based outcome isn't universally achieved across MetroLacrosse's teams. Each coach implements the curriculum presented to them and activates the training they receive through their own individual filter. Their experience as a lacrosse player, their background in coaching,

12 What Is Sport System Re-Design?

their ability to relate to and work with youth, as well as many other variables, all affect the way the coach coaches.

Beyond Stick Skills

At MetroLacrosse, an overarching goal is to influence each player's self-efficacy. In simple terms, self-efficacy is the belief that you can do something. And they hope that later on, the players' newfound sense of mastery from overcoming a difficult learning task might generalize to other parts of their lives. For Metro-Lacrosse kids, and all kids for that matter, learning new things can seem intimidating and difficult. But because sport can give us such a safe environment to practice skills, it's fertile ground for changing our sense of self-efficacy in one task or domain at a time.

Noted psychologist Albert Bandura (1997) explains that the sources for building a resolute sense of self-efficacy include *performance accomplishment*—seeing evidence that you have succeeded; *vicarious learning*—watching and learning from others; and *verbal persuasion*—hearing positive statements from trusted others (including even self-persuasion). MetroLacrosse believes that one of the ways that the kids in their programs will develop self-efficacy is if coaches help them witness their own progress and focus on that *progress* instead of absolute performance.

And just as with stick skills, MetroLacrosse trains its coaches in this philosophy and provides curriculum that helps coaches find opportunities to put this philosophy into practice. But just as with players' stick skills, MetroLacrosse finds that some coaches do what they are trained to do, but many coaches don't. Accordingly, some players benefit, and some do not.

At the core, Sport System Re-Design (SSRD) is about giving MetroLacrosse another way to obtain both these outcomes: the stick skills and the growing sense of self-efficacy. This isn't to say that MetroLacrosse should stop doing coach education or writing curriculum. On the contrary, SSRD is about filling in the gaps where coach education and curriculum fall short, so that the three approaches might work together to have maximum impact. It's about helping MetroLacrosse overcome the individual differences that each coach brings, thereby creating an environment that consistently points kids towards the outcomes they want, whether those outcomes are better stick skills or a deeper sense of self-efficacy for their kids.

Changing the Game Itself

Whereas coach education focuses on the capacity of the coach to effect change in a player, and curriculum focuses on the power of thoughtfully organized learning activities and lessons to effect change, SSRD turns to the game itself, to the arrangement of interrelated elements of the sport system to effect change. It involves looking at the actual structure and design of the whole sport experience and purposefully altering elements of the game that we usually consider fixed. What's unique about the elements that we examine in SSRD is that they are aspects of the sport experience that are universal to everyone involved—the coaches, players, referees and fans. Making changes to these aspects of the game means changing the sport experience for everyone; it becomes impossible for participants to "not do" that aspect of the game. If the right changes are identified, all participants get the benefit of that change.

Before we go any further, it's important to introduce working definitions of some core concepts:

- **Sport System**: The sum total of all the core elements of the sport experience, including, but not limited to, the location or venue, equipment and gear, practices, competition, rules of play, participants (players, coaches, fans, referees, other teams, etc.) and the structures that support the play.
- **Outcome**: A specific goal you want to achieve through the sport experience. The thing that you are intending for participants to do, know, learn or think because of their participation in the sport experience.
- **Re-Design**: Thinking about the sport in a new way that leads to experimenting with and making changes to discrete elements in your sport system in order to achieve a specific outcome.

Using the terms defined above, Sport System Re-Design (SSRD) can be defined as follows: re-Designing the sport experience to get a desired outcome by changing or tinkering with core elements of the sport system.

Changing the Seemingly Unchangeable

What, exactly, are we talking about here? Let's consider basketball. Whether you are player, coach, spectator, referee or cheerleader, there are some things about basketball that are always the same, no matter what level of basketball you play, coach or watch. You can expect that people will be dribbling the ball instead of holding and running with it. There will be a hoop, a ball, and some area in space designated for the game. There will be players on two sides trying to get the ball into their hoops. There will probably be someone making "calls" about what is allowable and what isn't allowable in the game. These elements, universal and commonly understood things about the game, are the targets of SSRD. And they are targeted exactly because they are so commonly understood and abided by.

The goal of SSRD is to look at the things that are seemingly unchangeable in a sport and put in place changes that would better serve the outcome we want to achieve. For example, if the goal is to make golf accessible for younger kids, then as SSRD practitioners, we might suggest giving them a shorter club that's easier to swing. We might move their tee closer to the hole so they don't have to hit the ball as far. Or, we might even put much bigger holes into our golf course so that it is easier for players who are just learning to control their clubs and balls to get the ball in the hole.

14 What Is Sport System Re-Design?

If a soccer program were to ask an SSRD practitioner how to ensure that all the games that their participants play are evenly matched, the SSRD practitioner might suggest that instead of playing two 45-minute *halves*, the program schedule two 45-minute *games* during that time. That way, the score and the teams can reset after the first game and have a chance to be victorious in the second. And if one team is considerably better than the other, games that end 3–0 and 4–1 may seem more in reach and less discouraging than one game that ends 7–1. Less discouragement could result in players playing harder to the end of the match. An SSRD practitioner might also suggest that teams wear reversible jerseys so that team rosters can be shuffled at half-time to have more parity in the second half. After all, making the sides even is what kids will often do in pick-up games without prompting or adult supervision. Finally, an SSRD practitioner might suggest that the league rules be changed so that every time a team is winning by two or more goals, that team has to take one player off the field.

The Five Domains of SSRD

The above examples highlight changes to elements in sports that are often considered fixed. These elements of sport, these things that everyone usually takes for granted, fall into five categories. We call them the "five domains" of SSRD.[1] They are:

- **Playing space**: The physical layout of the space.
- **Equipment**: The gear used to play the sport.
- **Rules of the game**: Guidelines that dictate what you can and can't do before, during and after the run of play.
- **Rules of the league**: The structure around the games, the way the teams are organized, the rules teams follow throughout a season or year.
- **Roles**: The responsibilities of any of the stakeholders involved with the game, including but not limited to players, coaches, referees and fans.

It's important to understand how this methodology is different from the current ways that youth sports practitioners think about changing the game— through curriculum and coach education. Using our MetroLacrosse example, we can examine the differences between coach education, curriculum and SSRD:

Coach Education in MetroLacrosse: As we saw above, MetroLacrosse has invested a lot of time and energy in training their coaches to give good instruction so that they can help their players develop strong stick skills.

Curriculum in MetroLacrosse: To achieve the same goal, they have written curriculum that includes myriad drills and activities that help kids learn these skills. The activities in the curriculum are prioritized at the beginning of the season and are accompanied by step-by-step directions so coaches know exactly how the activities should be implemented.

Sport System Re-Design in MetroLacrosse: If MetroLacrosse wanted to develop their players' stick skills using SSRD, they might consider any of the following strategies across at least three domains:

- Modifying the **Equipment**: In lacrosse, goalkeepers have larger pockets on their sticks. What if all beginners used goalkeeper sticks so that they have larger pockets? Wouldn't that be a way that every coach could help beginners see more success in catching and holding the ball in the pocket?
- Changing the **Rules of the Game**: Or what if, in every MetroLacrosse game, kids who dropped the ball while running down the field were able to stop, pick it up, and keep going without the threat of a player from the other team scooping it up?
- Changing the **Rules of the League**: Like in Brian McCormick's Playmakers basketball league (described in the Introduction), what if lacrosse games in the entire "beginners" division were played three on three with one goal and one goalkeeper? Wouldn't that mean more touches with the stick and, therefore, additional opportunities to improve this vital skill?

Let's look at another example—USA Football: a youth sport organization that uses coach education and curriculum to achieve its outcomes, but is now facing another challenge. The football community is now mobilizing to respond to the research about player safety at all levels of the game. As more evidence points to the devastating impact that concussions can have on the brain, people at all levels of the football community have been looking at ways to minimize the number of player concussions and other head injuries. USA Football has done this through all three approaches—coach education, curriculum and Sport System Re-Design.

Coach Education in USA Football: Through USA Football's "Head's Up" initiative, coaches receive training in concussion recognition and response, proper equipment fitting, strategies for teaching the "Head's Up tackling and blocking techniques," heat preparedness, proper hydration and recognition of the signs of sudden cardiac arrest. Many leagues, and even states, are now requiring that youth football coaches receive this certification.

Curriculum in USA Football: "Head's Up" also provides a curriculum of activities that youth can do to practice techniques that will help keep them safe while tackling and blocking.

Sport System Re-Design in USA Football: USA Football has made changes to the game in order to try to minimize the number of concussions per season by working with two domains:

- Changing the **Rules of the Game**: In 2013, a rule change stated that "at least four members of a kickoff team must be on each side of the kicker. This prohibits a kicking team from bunching up ... to create significant

16 What Is Sport System Re-Design?

mismatches when trying to recover a free kick."[2] This is intended to protect players from concussion.

- Changing the **Equipment**: Advances in technology spurred changes to helmets. An example of this newsworthy shift is reported by USA Today: "Riddell, official helmet maker of the NFL and a co-defendant in the concussion lawsuits, is introducing this season a sensor system in the helmet that transmits when impacts exceed a player's history on hits, geared for youth and high school teams."[3]

Re-Design Is at the League Level

Sport System Re-Design is about putting into place things that everyone must adhere to—whether it is playing with the same equipment, following the same rules or engaging in the game through a prescribed role. In order for this to be true, changes to the game have to be administered at a "league" level. This is part of what makes SSRD unique and powerful. SSRD makes changes to the things about the game that all the participants in a certain league collectively agree *are* part of the game. SSRD is not one coach giving players goalkeeper sticks during practice to help them learn skills, because once that coach brings the team to a game, they'll have to change back to regular sticks. In order for that equipment change to really be SSRD, it has to be something that is implemented during the *game*. In order for this to be true, it has to be part of the *league* in which the team plays.

Real SSRD means that somewhere a league administrator upholds that their sport will be played in a certain way in their league. And that there are consequences for any person involved in the league not playing the game that certain way. The reason why limiting the number of players that can be on one side of the kicker works is because it's something that everyone has to do. If they don't, the referee will make them kick it again. And they may even be penalized because of it.

So SSRD provides a more consistent and universal strategy than educating coaches about the benefits of touchbacks and hoping coaches encourage more of them in the course of play. A good practitioner of SSRD is always thinking about how to make a change in the game become seamlessly integrated as a "part of the game."

Re-Design Is About Outcomes

The next and most important thing a good practitioner of SSRD needs is to know what they're designing for. They have to always have in mind the *outcome* that they are trying to achieve. We have seen that one great feature of the SSRD approach is that the methodology can be used to achieve any outcome that can be achieved through youth sports. This includes, but is not limited to, results like these: facilitating more access to sport, creating an environment that is inclusive of athletes with disabilities, increasing participation of an underrepresented group, achieving parity between teams so that kids are benefitting from playing with and against other kids of similar ability, enhancing skill development, promoting character and life skills, and increasing physical fitness.

The outcomes we can re-Design for in sports can also be a great first step for achieving broader outcomes that the sports environment can't directly bring about. A prime example of this came up at one of our conferences. A participant asked if SSRD could help us use sport to solve world hunger. While this would be quite a stretch, we do know that there are lots of things that sport can do to create the *kinds of people* who could solve world hunger—the sorts of people that as a result of transformational sport experiences are more empathetic, work well in a team, give great effort and are committed to a goal. And SSRD can help us do that better than we are currently doing. For example, if we look for an attribute that we can develop in people to make them more likely to care about people who don't have enough to eat, we might land on the attribute of empathy or on the development of helping behaviors. These characteristics could be viewed as outcomes we seek for the participants in a given league or program.

What would our league look like if we re-Designed for empathy? Maybe we'd want every player to have the chance to play with other players, so we might use Dean Conway's JP Youth Soccer re-Design (described in the Introduction) on the structure of teams. Or, what if we could modify the scoring so that teams that showed the most empathetic behaviors—helping people up when they fall down, exhibiting good sportsmanship, etc.—would receive extra points?

While it is great to be able to use this methodology to design for any outcome, as youth sports practitioners, we actually know that there are outcomes that we *should* design for. These are outcomes that have a deeper impact on the positive youth development of the players we coach. They are the "high leverage" outcomes that we really should be pointing our coach education, curriculum and SSRD towards. These high-leverage outcomes include the following:

- **Physical Activity**: Getting 60 minutes of moderate to vigorous physical activity a day (MVPA) can help promote physical health and ensure the physiological and psycho-emotional benefits of decreasing stress and relaxation.
- **Parity of Competition**: Parity in competition is a value supported by the research on "flow" and optimal experience (Csikszentmihalyi, 2014). According to theories of engagement, the ideal conditions for optimal experience are when the challenge is appropriately matched with the level of skill.
- **Participation and Retention**: These two outcomes are inextricably intertwined. If children or youth participate and get a lot of chances, they usually get better and have more enjoyment. When they improve it is motivating, and that can help them decide to want to continue playing.
- **Sport Skill Building**: In every sport there are key skills that are essential to be successful in a game. The ability to throw, run, catch, shoot, tackle, pass, etc., are things that ensure success and a sense of confidence that can be brought into the more challenging situation of a competition.

18 What Is Sport System Re-Design?

- **Life Skill Building**: This is the ultimate quest of sport-based youth development programs. Although all youth sport programs aim to develop things like courage, honesty, determination, fairness, respect, etc., it is difficult to do this. How can we use our tools to better achieve this important but elusive outcome?

If all of our sports achieved these things, our sports environments would be producing physically fit, competent athletes of good character who make health-seeking decisions. If we can achieve these outcomes, we can finally begin to deliver on the promise of sport. In the next chapter, we'll dive deeper into the SSRD methodology by exploring the five domains and looking at the process for implementing re-Design in your program. In Chapter 3, we'll provide a rationale for why this work is increasingly important in the U.S. and beyond. Finally, in Chapter 4, we're going to explore the concept of re-Design further by looking at the roots of the methodology, sources and inspirations both inside and outside of sport that have influenced this work.

Notes

1. These categories overlap in part with those proposed independently by the Competitive Engineering group (see Burton et al. 2011a, 2011b).
2. USA Football Rules Committee approves three rule changes for youth football rule book. (2012, November 20). Retrieved April 27, 2015, from http://usafootball.com/news/press-box/usa-football-rules-committee-approves-three-rule-changes-youth-football-rule-book#sthash.o0mmFHam.dpuf.
3. Mihoces, G. (2013, August 23). More padding the issue of concussions and better helmets. USA Today. Retrieved April 27, 2015, from www.usatoday.com/story/sports/ncaaf/2013/07/30/concussions-college-football-nfl-guardian-caps/2601063/.

References

Bandura, A. (1997). *Self-efficacy: The exercise of control.* New York: W.H. Freeman and Company.

Burton, D., O'Connell, K., Gillham, A. D., & Hammermeister, J. (2011a). More cheers and fewer tears: Examining the impact of competitive engineering on scoring and attrition in youth flag football. *International Journal of Sports Science and Coaching, 6*(2), 219–228.

Burton, D., Gillham, A., & Hammermeister, J. (2011b). Competitive engineering: Structural climate modifications to enhance youth athletes' competitive experience. *International Journal of Sports Science and Coaching, 6*(2), 201–218.

Csikszentmihalyi, M. (2014). *Flow.* The Netherlands: Springer.

Mihoces, G. (2013, August 23). More padding the issue of concussions and better helmets. USA Today. Retrieved April 27, 2015, from www.usatoday.com/story/sports/ncaaf/2013/07/30/concussions-college-football-nfl-guardian-caps/2601063/.

USA Football Rules Committee approves three rule changes for youth football rule book. (2012, November 20). Retrieved April 27, 2015, from http://usafootball.com/news/press-box/usa-football-rules-committee-approves-three-rule-changes-youth-football-rule-book#sthash.o0mmFHam.dpuf.

2

THE FIVE DOMAINS OF SPORT SYSTEM RE-DESIGN

In this chapter we provide detailed explanations of each of the five domains introduced in Chapter 1, and provide actual examples of re-Designs in each domain. But before that, we want to briefly describe the impetus for our use of these five domains as organizing principles in SSRD. It all started with a unique project Lou was working on in 2009.

Lou was working with a Boston-based, multi-sport, year-round program—the Doc Wayne Youth Services (DWYS)—that is deeply committed to impacting their players outside of sport. As he crafted their unique curriculum and worked to train their coaches, he also spent a great deal of time watching the league. It was not high-level sport relative to other more mainstream competitive leagues, yet the opportunities for skill building and life-skill development were remarkable.

Because this population—adolescent girls affected by complex trauma—had very specific needs, the DWYS league administrators had gone to great lengths to tweak, bend and reinvent some of the rules of each of the four sports they played.

- In *basketball*, though it was full-court play, teams were only permitted to play half-court defense. Full-court defense had proven too stressful for the players and with their lower skill level, it had been too difficult for some players and teams to even get the ball to half court.
- In *flag football*, they opted for a coach-as-quarterback. The coach played the entire game—calling plays, organizing the offense and with the help of additional coaches, making all of the substitutions.
- In *softball*, the safety base was utilized. This is a double-wide first base that allows base runners and the first base field player to stand farther away from each other. A coach was allowed to stand near second base to assist and instruct runners.

20 Five Domains of Sport System Re-Design

- In *soccer*, substitutions were unlimited and if the referee thought both teams needed a rest, he would pause the game for teams to come together and regroup.

Each of these tweaks was created to try to get something more out of the competitive experience for the players. And because this league was working with such a special population, nobody really ever questioned whether these sport system changes were somehow violating the "spirit of the game" or wondered whether this version of the sport was somehow "less than" what other kids were playing. The modifications became just "the way we do things here."

As Lou began to work with the DWYS league administrators and coaches to make some additional intentional changes, something powerful began to happen. Lou attended the weekly games, and as he would run from court to court to encourage the coaches to implement the new curriculum, he logged a lot of hours just watching the sports. Week after week, he would talk with the league administrators before games, watch them during the games (they often worked as the referees/umpires) and debrief with them at the end of the evening. They would wrestle with how to solve some of the challenges that would surface during the course of a season, like:

- Some offensive players would feel threatened by the proximity of a defending player and react in extreme, sometimes violent, ways to protect themselves.
- Some players lacked the coordination to stop their body quickly or make cutting turns and would collide with players from the other teams.
- For some players, despite being visibly affected by the stress of the game, they couldn't get off the field/court of play until there was an official substitution.

Without articulating it, Lou came to the conclusion that coach education and curriculum were not solving these issues. Thus the idea of "league-level intervention" was born. At that time, he did not have the vocabulary for what he was trying to do, nor did he have a framework of "domains" around which to organize the interventions. There was just a deep desire to achieve certain outcomes, often related to emotional and physical safety or skill building, and a group of league administrators and coaches who were deeply committed to doing whatever it took to get those outcomes. Everyone was on the same page that the outcomes mattered much more than whether or not it looked like "real basketball" or "real soccer." In other words, there was a deep commitment to experimenting with the sport itself.

With this energy and commitment, Lou, the DWYS league administrators, the coaches and the players embarked on a multi-season series of experiments. Quickly, the concept of "league-level intervention" took shape, and it became apparent that an adjustment to the structure of the sport itself could produce a dramatic impact.

Over the next few years, what we initially called "League-Level Intervention" evolved into "Sport System Re-Design." During this time, our team of John, Lou and Megan came together around work Megan was doing at Up2Us Sports. The conversations about re-Design started to go deeper and we realized we were building something that was not just a collection of interesting approaches to getting outcomes through sport. By discovering and cataloguing how others had re-designed their sports, we were building a new pathway for impact. And this pathway had the potential to positively impact the lives of everyone involved in youth sport.

We recently learned that in 2011, as we planned our first SSRD conference for league administrators, another group independently came up with a framework called Competitive Engineering (CE) that outlined changing areas of the game to achieve specific outcomes (Burton et al. 2011a, 2011b). We believe this parallel development validates the need for our approach. That academics, thought leaders, organizational consultants and practitioners are converging on similar concepts is a good sign that the time is ripe for Sport System Re-Design.

The rest of this chapter describes in detail a comprehensive taxonomy to classify and understand how SSRD can manifest inside your sport system. In this chapter we will describe the five core domains of SSRD and provide re-Design examples from various sports. At the end of this chapter, we will describe several particularly powerful re-Designs that were born from the sport league that Lou worked with in Boston.

As previously mentioned, the five domains of Sport System Re-Design are:

1. **Playing Space**: The dimensions of and demarcations within the area of play
2. **Equipment**: Any items or resources utilized inside a sport to enable or enhance play
3. **Rules of the Game**: The set of explicit regulations that govern how the sport is played
4. **Rules of the League**: The set of explicit regulations and structures that govern how the league of the sport and competition between teams/players are conducted
5. **Roles**: The prescribed functions of all the major participants in a sport system, including players, coaches, fans and referees

These five domains are present in any sport system, regardless of whether it is a sport played on a field, a rink or on a mountain; a team or individual sport; or a sport of many or only a few competitors.

This "domain structure" provides a simple and comprehensive way to deconstruct a sport, examine each of its pillars, and then intentionally build it back up into something better, with different rules, unique roles, newly engineered equipment or even re-imagined playing spaces. A practitioner of SSRD has the opportunity to tinker and experiment with re-Designs in any of these five domains in order to change the game in a way that helps them achieve their desired outcome.

SSRD Domain #1: Re-Design the *Playing Space*

This domain of re-Design has to do with altering the physical environment or setting in which we play our sport. This setting could be a field, court, rink, pool, park, slope, river, beach, etc. Many of us have experience changing the playing space in a practice setting. For example, in soccer, we create grids on our fields for small-sided games to force more footwork. A re-Design of playing space considers what would happen if the space was shrunken, widened, lengthened, deepened or somehow otherwise changed, as shown in the examples below.

Indoor Soccer and Futsal

Indoor soccer and futsal are variations of the traditional outdoor game in which the field is significantly smaller. Indoor soccer is often played on a turf field the size of a hockey rink, and futsal is played on an even smaller field. The smaller field forces players to better develop their ball control and precision passing skills because of the tighter quarters and additional touches on the ball.

Cross-Ice Hockey

Cross-Ice Hockey is an innovation described in detail in our Case Studies section. The creators of cross-ice hockey set up two or three side-by-side hockey rinks inside a traditional regulation hockey rink, making the size of each playing area smaller. The result has been more touches on the puck, increased decision-making practice, more chances to score, and additional opportunities to work on starting and stopping and changes of direction. In short, there is much more skill building during the small-sided games than there was in the full-sized rink.

Snowboard Half-Pipe

Recently introduced, the snowboard half-pipe event is like skateboarding on a ski slope! Developers retained the "bowl" concept of a half-pipe and just extended its length all the way down the ski slope so that a snowboarder could retain speed and momentum.

Circuit Road Race Routes

Watching running events in a stadium is exciting because spectators can see the entire race unfold. Long-distance road race organizers have borrowed a chapter from this concept and designed races that follow a circuit or loop route. This means that spectators can view racers multiple times, there is a better atmosphere for the runners because supporters aren't as spread out, and the race hosts are less inconvenienced because fewer roads need to be shut down.

SSRD Domain #2: Re-Design the *Equipment*

When we talk about equipment, we refer to any and all items or gear related to your sport. In each sport, a specific set of equipment is used. This equipment is often strictly regulated to improve safety, consistency and performance. The most familiar re-Design that happens in almost every sport is the "right-sizing" of equipment for different age groups. Soccer balls and basketballs, skis and snowboards, tennis racquets and tennis balls are right-sized for the age and size of the player. Equipment re-Designs are also core to many adapted sports, which make it possible for differently abled players to participate, such as wheelchairs for rugby, sleds for hockey, and electronic sounds inside baseballs.

Because sport equipment is closely regulated by governing bodies in sport and is reliant on the sporting goods manufacturers, we often do not think that we can re-Design equipment. Yet, some of the most important re-Designs come from changes to equipment. Consider the following examples.

Tee-ball

Tee-ball is a hugely popular developmental version of baseball and softball built around one very simple, yet profound re-Design: the ball sitting on top of a stand for younger players so that they have a much better chance of hitting the ball.

Helmets and Pads in Football

There was a time when football was played with a leather helmet and no pads. Equipment re-Design has been at the center of the evolution of football and has resulted in making the game much safer. As the NFL works to address the current crisis around concussions, equipment re-Design is again at the center of its attempts to make the sport even safer.

The Wheelchair

We often think of the wheelchair only as a piece of equipment that creates access to movement in the lives of people with different abilities. Yet the wheelchair has been at the center of the adapted sports movement for decades. People have been tinkering with wheelchair design to engineer many different variations that allow athletes with disabilities to compete in numerous sports including, but not limited to, wheelchair basketball, quad rugby, marathons, tennis, fencing and even downhill mountain biking.

Vanishing Foam in Professional Soccer

In the 2014 World Cup in Brazil, FIFA debuted one of the most innovative equipment re-Designs that soccer has ever seen: it is dubbed by many the "magic foam." When a team is awarded a free kick, the defending team

24 Five Domains of Sport System Re-Design

must stand 10 yards away. Historically, referees would walk off the 10 yards, and the defending team would line up where the referee pointed. But as soon as the referee stepped away, defending players would often take small steps forward until the ball was kicked, gaining an unfair advantage on defense. It has been one of the most nagging problems in soccer, until now. Referees now carry a small can of spray foam on their person. They walk off the 10 yards and then spray a line on the ground. There can now be no dispute as to where defending players must stand. The foam dissolves in a few minutes and leaves no marks on the field. Equipment re-Design = problem solved!

Modified Shot Clocks in Basketball

Game clocks in the NBA and college basketball were the first to implement LED light strips on the edges of the clock so that, as time expires, you not only hear a buzzer go off, but you see the lights on the side of the clock illuminate. This helps players and referees determine if they got the shot off in time to count as a basket.

SSRD Domain #3: Re-Design the *Rules of the Game*

This domain typically encompasses the widest range of potential re-Designs, because most sports have an extensive set of regulations and mandates around how the sport is played. The longer and more detailed the rule book is for a sport, the greater the opportunities available to us to consider a wide range of re-Designs. Oftentimes, even small changes in this domain can have a profound effect on many elements of the sport and how it is played.

Some of the most common rule re-Designs that are present in multiple sports include the following: player eligibility, restrictions on substitutions, how points are scored, and what are considered rule violations.

We often forget that changing the rules is a common strategy that coaches use during practice to get the outcomes they want. They create temporary rules around number of passes before a shot can be taken. They force certain types of substitutions. They temporarily declare certain kinds of play either fair or foul play. They even assign point values to certain types of "scores." In other parts of the sports world, governing bodies consistently examine the game and make changes to how it is played.

Below are some examples:

3-Point Line in Basketball

Basketball is itself a sport that was built from scratch not too long ago. Since its inception, it has gone through some of the most significant re-Designs in the history of sport. Consider just some of its rule changes: the amount of time a team has to shoot and the invention of shot clocks, how possession came to be determined by jump ball, and the addition of the concept of team fouls. The 3-point line did not exist when basketball was invented. It was then introduced, taken out and is now an integral part of the game. Yet, even the 3-point line is a different distance in college and professional basketball.

The Mercy Rule

Typically, the mercy rule has been instituted to prevent games where the score is overwhelmingly lopsided. In some baseball and softball leagues, the rule comes into effect after a certain number of innings are played and the score differential exceeds a certain number. In NCAA softball, the rule is invoked if one team is outscoring their opponents by at least eight runs after five innings have been played. There is also a version of the mercy rule in amateur boxing. If a boxer is trailing his or her opponent by more than 20 points, the referee will stop the fight. There is even a mercy rule in high school basketball in some states in the U.S.: if a team is winning by more than 35 points in the second half, the game clock runs continuously and is only stopped for officials' timeouts or injury timeouts and the end of the third quarter.

Kick-off Line in Football

The NFL has moved the kick-off line five yards closer in an attempt to reduce the number of kickoff returns and to shorten the distance between tacklers and runners. The kickoff return has proven to be one of the most high-risk plays in football, with players colliding and resulting in numerous injuries. This rule makes it more likely for a kicker to be able to kick the ball into or beyond the end zone, thus resulting in the inability of a player to run the kick up the field.

Sudden Victory in Wrestling

In 2004, the NCAA incorporated a new overtime format called "sudden victory" for matches that end in a tie. This period starts with both wrestlers in a neutral standing position. Then the first wrestler to score a "takedown" wins.

SSRD Domain #4: Re-Design the *Rules of the League*

At every level, from professional sports to community-based recreation programs, leagues are governed by a set of rules that provide structure for how teams will interact with each other during the course of a particular season. League

26 Five Domains of Sport System Re-Design

rules commonly define eligibility of certain players, lengths of a season of play, tournament structure, etc. Professional and college leagues often tinker with league rules to achieve more parity between teams and to create the most exciting playoff format. For example, NCAA Division I college football just recently shifted to a playoff format, after having had a different end-of-season structure for decades. The NFL and MLB have added "wild card" teams so that more teams make the playoffs. And NCAA college basketball has a single-elimination tournament structure, while the NBA plays a series of matches to determine which teams advance.

Here are more examples of Rules re-Designs:

Professional Soccer's "Division" Format

The English Premier League moves teams through a series of linked divisions, depending on their performance. At the end of each season, teams at the bottom of each division are relegated to a lower division for the next season. Teams at the top of each division advance into the higher division for the next season. This model promotes match parity as teams spend their season playing other teams of similar competitiveness while also vying to advance to the next division for the next season.

Off-the-Field Factors Influence League Standings

MYSA, the Mathare Youth Sports Association, located in one of the largest slums in Kenya (and the only youth sports program ever nominated for a Nobel Prize), takes a unique approach to their league standings. Teams compete on the field and earn points for wins, losses and ties. Additionally, teams participate in neighborhood cleanups in their community, and their time spent doing this community work is counted as points in their league standings.

First-to-Arrive, First-to-Play

Like Dean Conway's JP Youth Soccer league (see Introduction), there are several youth sports leagues that have moved away from fixed teams in their sport season and instead adopt this approach of "first-to-arrive, first-to-play." All players are given a reversible jersey at the beginning of the season (Equipment re-Design!) and, when they arrive on competition day, are immediately sent to the first open playing space and assigned to a team. As soon as that playing space and the supervising referee have enough players to play, that competition begins. The players that arrive after are sent to the second playing space to play and so forth. As the competition day progresses, teams may rotate to different playing spaces, and players may even change teams, all to maximize playing time and parity of play. And throughout the competition, players simply reverse their jerseys to be able to play on either team.

Change Teams and Keep Your Points

Cross Cultures, a European-based sport for development program, has a unique approach to tournament play. Each player is assigned a number and a team for their first match. After each match, players are randomly shuffled to new teams and meet on a new playing space to compete together. A coach uses a special chart to assign points to each player based on whether their team won, lost or tied the previous competition, just as you would for a team, but instead, individual players earn these points. In this way, players get to play matches with many different peers, no team can dominate a tournament because teams are constantly being reconstituted and at the end of the tournament, individual players who played on the most winning teams are recognized instead of teams.

SSRD Domain #5: Re-Design *the Roles*

This re-Design specifically targets the key people involved in your sport system and how they can play the most productive and positive role possible. This includes coaches, referees, players and fans. Typically, we assign roles during games based on how roles are divided at the professional or collegiate level. We think a referee must follow a certain set of behaviors, or coaches can or cannot do certain things. When we allow ourselves to shatter these preconceptions, we can adapt current roles and even invent new roles that can dramatically change the impact that the sport can have on our players.

This domain of re-Design involves thinking creatively about how to define the roles for each of these key people in our sport system.

Consider the following examples:

Coach as Pitcher

In youth baseball and softball, once players graduate from Tee-ball, they often play with the coach as the full-time pitcher. The coach is more likely to throw consistent pitches over the plate and can often adjust the pitch to increase the chances that players will make contact when they swing. In this role, the coach has a much greater chance of promoting player development and skill building for the individual players and the entire team.

Referee/Umpire as Teacher

The referee/umpire in many sports is the one who is closest to the play and because of that proximity can engage in a certain type of dialogue with

28   Five Domains of Sport System Re-Design

players that other adults can't. There are leagues where the referee is not only encouraged, but expected, to teach the game while it is being played. If there is a rule violation, especially a persistent one, the referee will stop and explain a rule or its intent, so as to help the players not only abide by the rule but to understand why it is a rule that promotes fair play.

Spectators as "Boundaries"

Triton Youth Soccer Association has come up with a truly creative way to solve two challenges at once: over-zealous parents and stoppage of play due to too many balls going out of bounds. For their youngest age soccer matches, they assign parents to locations around the field. Parents must stand watch at their station and if a ball is kicked towards them that is going out of bounds, they simply and gently kick it to keep it in play. In essence, they are serving as human bumpers!

Spectators Support Opposing Team

Knowing that their opponents didn't have a fan base, a high school basketball team in Texas reassigned half of their fans to support the opposing team. These fans wore the opposing team's colors and filled the gym with cheers and support—for the other team! Most competitions are better when both teams/competitors have real support from the crowd. A re-Design mindset allows you to redefine what "home team fan" really means.

Player as Referee

FIFA is supporting the implementation of a version of youth soccer they call "Fair Play." In Fair Play soccer, there are no referees, and players make their own calls as well as resolve disputed calls. This type of soccer promotes more dialogue, conflict resolution and player ownership for the way the game is played. Another example: Ultimate Frisbee, from the intramural to the professional and international levels, has no referees. Players make their own calls in every instance.

As we've seen in this chapter, there are so many ways to change the game. With so many possibilities it can be hard to start our own re-Design work. That's why we've created the domain framework. It provides us with a way to organize around the possible change we want to make in order to get the outcomes we wish to achieve.

We hope that the examples in this chapter have helped bring the five domains to life. More than that, we hope that they have helped debunk the commonly held belief that our sports are static. Instead, sports are constantly being tweaked to achieve certain outcomes. It's just that the outcomes that we've been seeking are not the ones we, as practitioners of sports-based youth development, want.

Five Domains of Sport System Re-Design **29**

But if the methodology of changing the game works for those outcomes, why not the ones we want? Why can't we change the equipment or the rules so that we can help kids get more physical activity? Why can't we think about the roles of the people involved in the game if it means we can help kids develop their sport and life skills? Why are we so resistant to changing the game so that we encourage more kids to play?

Lou was lucky that the program he worked with in 2009 was willing to dismiss all notions of what sport "should be" in exchange for what sports "can be." The examples below outline some of the most innovative re-Designs that have come out of that program.

- Players call timeouts, and timeouts are unlimited—This allows players to feel like they are in control of the game because when they get overwhelmed, they can call a timeout without hurting their team. In a similar way, it helps their coaches to be able to protect their player from situations that could be too stressful.
- Possession arrow in soccer—In a situation in which a collision between two players is accidental, instead of calling a foul, the referee alternately awards possession; borrowing the concept of the possession arrow in basketball and applying it to soccer.
- Referees join timeouts and team huddles during the game—This is designed to get players and coaches to see the referees as allies. Further, it enables referees to have a chance to interact with the teams, educate them about rules, and have a calming dialogue with them and the coaches.

It's time for all youth sports to be as creative and innovative as this program. It's the only way we'll be able to change the youth sports experience from what it "should be" able to deliver into something that absolutely "can be" a transformative experience for youth.

In the next chapter we provide a rationale for this approach. Chapter 4 provides a look at sources of inspiration both inside and outside of sport. And in the next section of the book, the SSRD toolkit will provide you with all that you need to make these changes in your own sport system.

References

Burton, D., O'Connell, K., Gillham, A. D., & Hammermeister, J. (2011a). More cheers and fewer tears: Examining the impact of competitive engineering on scoring and attrition in youth flag football. *International Journal of Sports Science and Coaching, 6*(2), 219–228.

Burton, D., Gillham, A., & Hammermeister, J. (2011b). Competitive engineering: Structural climate modifications to enhance youth athletes' competitive experience. *International Journal of Sports Science and Coaching, 6*(2), 201–218.

3

WHY CHANGE THE GAME . . .
AND WHY NOW?

Recall in our Introduction we told the story of Dean Conway's revamping of youth soccer and Brian McCormick's changes to youth basketball. These stories may be inspiring to some, but for others they may raise the question, *so what?* Why should these examples convince parents, coaches, teachers and athletes to think about re-designing their game? And why should we be concerned with changing the game *now*?

In this chapter we'll present the argument that in fact, there are currently many reasons to consider changing the game, from the highest levels of professional sport to the local playground where parents congregate to watch their kids play Little League baseball. We'll start by describing a number of problems—some national, some local—that justify our attention to Sport System Re-Design and that provide a rationale for why this makes sense *now*.

The Commissioner of Baseball Has a Problem

Like the leadership of any large corporation, the commissioner and his advisors must stay on top of trends that can be promising or threatening to the continued success of their business. The time-honored sport of baseball used to occupy an important place in our collective psyche as "America's Pastime." And while the financial status of baseball is still robust—there are still big television contracts and lucrative player compensation—viewership is down. Knowing that a healthy following is the only way to stay relevant, Major League Baseball (MLB) is already examining ways to speed up the game in order to attract more support.

The future of baseball is further threatened by trends at the grassroots level. Back in the 1990s, an MLB scout named John Young noted trouble ahead for baseball with the disappearance of games, teams and leagues, particularly in

32 Why Change the Game?

urban centers. He observed the decay of baseball facilities, safe spaces and the infrastructure to support baseball being played in urban centers. While basketball was gaining status as a culturally important game, baseball was quietly slipping away. He realized that youth baseball in urban centers was in crisis and proposed a program to revive it. He believed that the best way to bring baseball back to South Central LA was to introduce a comprehensive youth baseball program for 13- to 16-year-olds. In 1991, the Commissioner of Major League Baseball started funding a program called RBI, Reviving Baseball in the Inner Cities. In Young's words, RBI would provide "disadvantaged youth an opportunity to learn and enjoy the game of baseball."[1]

While there are many vibrant programs that have grown in this model, the current MLB Commissioner might wonder whether what happened in the inner cities in the 1990s was emblematic of a much bigger problem—opportunities and resources to play might not be the only reasons that baseball had been losing ground. It may also be that the game itself is not as compelling to young people as it once was. The pace of the game may now seem glacial to Generation X and Millennials, who are used to the information-heavy, instantly gratifying world made possible by advances in technology.

Consider for a moment that in the 1960s and 1970s big innovations and fads were the game "Twister" and the "Hula Hoop." What were once the hottest games that could be found in basements across the country like table top hockey or foosball or even ping-pong, have been replaced by high-tech, highly engaging (if not addictive) video games that are pushing the boundaries of virtual reality. What is more, many of these games can be played with other kids or other people across the world through the internet. Incredibly, all these opportunities can be accessed using a phone or other similar portable device.

Unlike the hula-hoop—a true fad—these sorts of technology are not fads; they are increasingly how all of us, especially young people, are connected to the world. While this may be a larger problem for all sports, baseball is particularly vulnerable to losing participants because the pace is slower than in other sports like lacrosse and ice hockey—where youth participation continues to rise.

If you doubt whether baseball has a problem in the US, take a look at who plays baseball in the Major Leagues. An increasing number of players come from outside of the United States: Cuba, Puerto Rico, Venezuela, the Dominican Republic and Japan. That their players are skilled enough to attract MLB scouts points to the fact that their countries are deeply invested in baseball. In contrast, Little League baseball in the U.S. has 25% fewer participants today than 15 years ago, a change many attribute to the slow pace of the game.[2]

Hockey Has a Problem

Hockey has also noticed problems inside their sport and has begun some significant attempts at re-Design. Years ago, when John coached football at Boston University, all the male sport coaches shared a common locker room. In this old-school locker room, coaches would commiserate about a tough loss or celebrate the success of another team even if their own team was struggling. They would talk about coaching, administrative woes and recruiting. John once asked the legendary men's Ice Hockey coach Jack Parker about recruiting in the Boston area. He said, "There are no players anymore. I used to go to towns like Saugus and Winchester and Malden and be able to find players." Puzzled, John asked him why he couldn't find players. He curtly replied, "Because the coaching stinks."

This seemed weird to John. Why would hockey coaching have gone downhill? It turned out Parker was referring to more global changes. He said, "Now the coaches try to control everything and teach their *own* systems, not sound, basic hockey. The kids are too busy being driven from one tournament to the next, and nobody has time to play on the ponds anymore. They don't have the skills that kids used to develop playing shinny hockey."

Coach Parker was actually referring to a complex set of problems, not simply bad coaching. "Shinny hockey" is the informal game of hockey played with just shin guards on ponds and in backyards all over the region. Why didn't kids still play hockey on ponds? Of course the same attractions pulling youth away from baseball could be implicated here. But in addition, the youth game itself had changed. Youth hockey, like other youth sports, had become much more adult-run: a good thing in some ways, but with unintended consequences. Now kids were being coached on the tactics of facing off or implementing special defensive traps rather than devoting time to actually skating, reacting, making passes and taking shots on goals.

This lesson is echoed by what we know of the hockey rinks of Finland and Sweden. Finland and Sweden routinely give the Team USA trouble. Their approach to "teaching" ice hockey is different than ours. Early on, it is said, they put 100 kids on the ice with 100 pucks. What happens? You quickly learn to keep your head up and not lose the puck amid the chaos created by those 99 other kids.

In Chapter 8, we'll describe how the leaders of USA Hockey, the national governing organization of youth hockey in the U.S., have identified some of the problems that have slowed talent development, including retention of players from the lowest levels. And we'll talk about how they have tried to address those issues.

The Commissioner of Football Has a Problem

While baseball still holds importance as America's Pastime, the National Football League (NFL) has taken its place in recent decades as "America's passion."[3] The NFL is popular for many reasons. In addition to the violent collisions that occur on almost every play, on average, there is great parity in the league; on any given Sunday most games are competitive. And then there is the culture that surrounds football, which includes team merchandise and apparel, tailgating, in-stadium entertainment, fantasy football and gambling.

34 Why Change the Game?

On the other hand, recently, player safety has risen into the public consciousness. This has happened before. Safety concerns in football are not new. For example, in the time of President Teddy Roosevelt, teams like Harvard and Princeton employed a tactic called the "Flying Wedge," which had players linking arms and charging towards oncoming defenders in a plow-like arrangement with crushing effect. This tactic was so dangerous that it resulted in 19 player deaths in 1932. Roosevelt convened the top leaders of college football at that time and banned the "Flying Wedge." In addition, they added penalties for unsportsmanlike conduct. At the same time they also introduced the forward pass and the neutral zone, which resulted in changing the game into the modern offensive game it is today.

The invention of plastic changed the face of football and has contributed to the intense focus on safety in the modern era. Lightweight but durable material has, since the 1960s, found its way into "protecting" football players from contact. It is undeniably true that the horrific skull crushing and face injuries that were common in the Flying Wedge era were prevented, and the efforts to protect the face and head of football players have been quite successful. Yet, unfortunately, this "protection" imbued players with a false sense of safety and security. Further, once players and coaches realized that wielding the helmet as a weapon could be used to a competitive advantage, the "weaponization" of the helmet evolved with deadly efficiency. In this struggle for a competitive edge, the silent long-term effects on the brains of the players employing these tactics were ignored.

The issue of brain injury challenges the viability of the game not only at the professional level but at every level, all the way down to youth football. Anyone close to the game of football has known for some time that football players were getting concussions. Coaches, parents and even medical personnel used to minimize the seriousness of being concussed by referring to it as getting your "bell rung" or "getting dinged." What has changed in the last 10 years is our understanding of the potential long-term consequences of concussions and thereby our sensitivity to their seriousness. The fact that the way the game is played dramatically increases the risk of traumatic brain injury can no longer be ignored.

As more and more research focuses on the problem of concussions, it seems that the NFL has an intractable problem. People seem to love to watch the big hits and mayhem that the NFL game delivers, but fans, coaches and owners collectively have to now question whether these hits are worth it.

My Neighbors Have a Problem . . . and So Do Their Kids!

The examples we've presented above center on talent development, waning interest in a specific sport, and health and safety issues. And these brief examples from professional sport show that every level of sport wrestles with problems that they would like to solve.

Why Change the Game? **35**

The case for re-Design, at the youth and community level, is as compelling as it is at the professional or elite realm. Here, we see problems that are just as important and just as much in need of change. Let's begin with a story about a neighbor of John's who is immersed in the world of youth sport.

A few years ago John became acquainted with a man named Peter. He is the sort of guy who probably feels in charge in most circumstances. He is well-educated, sends his six children to private schools, and by almost any standard would be considered wealthy. At that time, all of his children were involved in youth sport. He asked John, "Do you have any kids in youth sport?" At that point, the oldest of John's children was five years old. John answered, "Our kids aren't involved with any youth sports yet." Peter's tone changed, now sounding more like a fraternity brother who felt compelled to warn John about the initiation he was about to face, "You wait, it sucks!"

He then began to recount his current youth-sport-related misery to John. He explained, "Get ready, because you'll be stuck traveling from one practice or game to the next. And you will watch your children not play in favor of the less talented son or daughter of the coach of the travel team." He continued, "And start saving your money! Because you're going to need it to pay for the exorbitant costs of everything involved with the whole enterprise: the equipment, the registration fees, the camps, and that's just the beginning."

Then he asked, "Do you get along with your wife?" Unsure where he was headed with his line of inquiry, John replied, "Most of the time." He exclaimed, "Well, you can forget her too, because you have more than one child. Once you get involved you won't even see your wife anymore because you'll always be driving in different directions!"

When parents sign their child up for youth soccer, hockey, basketball or some other sport, what is it they hope for their child? Peter had an intense and mostly negative experience as a youth sports parent, which was clearly different than what he expected. Understanding parents' expectations, as well as player expectations, helps us pinpoint where sport isn't delivering on its promise. And where we might be able to tweak it to make it work for more parents and more kids.

Expectations for Physical Benefits

Let's begin with a core expectation, that "my child will get exercise if they participate in youth sport." This is clearly an important goal. One in three children in this country are overweight or obese.[4] The focus on high-stakes testing in schools means that time for formal physical education has been squeezed out of the schedule. Because of budget cuts and the pressures that No Child Left Behind legislation has imposed on school administrators, often they are forced to emphasize academic goals at the expense of physical activity during the school day. This means that many youth are not getting the recommended 60 minutes of moderate to vigorous physical activity (MVPA) during the school day.

36 Why Change the Game?

The situation is no better during out-of-school time. Participation fees keep more and more kids from accessing sports opportunities. Those youth who can afford to play are not guaranteed to continue. More than half of the youth who participate in non-school youth sports drop out by age 11.[5]

For those youth who do keep playing, there is no guarantee that they will get the MVPA they need. John discovered one of the reasons why while coaching his daughter's basketball team. After signing her up for their town's recreational team, John assumed that she would be getting some physical activity that would be good for her physical well-being. Basketball, played a few times a week—with all of the running up and down the court, playing defense, and cutting and moving to get open—seemed like an ideal sort of activity to reach at least moderate if not vigorous levels of activity, especially if John, an experienced coach, was coaching. Right?

Wrong. First, John discovered that due to the way the league was structured, after the first week of the preseason, the eight-game season would have a one-to-one ratio of practices to games. So they wouldn't actually be together very many times. Second, it turned out that there were fifteen girls on the team. Of course only five could play at a time. So two-thirds of the time the girls would be sitting on the bench waiting to play! Clearly this had huge implications for MVPA. John was so dismayed by this constraint that a few times during home games he brought jump ropes to allow the girls to get at least a bit of rigorous physical activity.

In the end it was the structure of the league and the numbers of girls on the team that actually stood in the way of the girls developing a basic level of fitness. John learned how difficult it was to ensure that he could deliver on his own basic assumption: that his daughter and the rest of the girls on the team would actually get moderate to vigorous physical activity from playing recreation basketball.

Expectations for Character Development

Beyond the health benefits, many parents expect that their children will get other positive social and emotional benefits from participating in sport—the development of character-enhancing dispositions such as leadership, teamwork, persistence and grit. Many parents hope that their child will experience social-emotional learning through sport, learning that will help them develop into caring and responsible adults. But youth sport has rightly come under public scrutiny, as it has become a site for controversy and egregious conduct, with many highly publicized events of fan, parent or player violence, sexual abuse, cheating, and an array of misguided coaching practices.

Many programs claim that they are devoutly focused on delivering character development to their participants. But when we dig deeper and look for evidence of this happening on the field, we rarely find it. As the children get older and competitiveness among the adults around the game gets more intense, what parents and coaches often model and teach to the participants is exactly opposite to these espoused values. Youth sports leagues rely on volunteers—who often have little or no training or education in coaching—and charge them with an unrealistic goal of creating an environment that fosters character development. Too many organizations make the wrong assumption that sport, by itself, is an environment that fosters character and don't attend to the fact that instead, it is something that has to be intentionally cultivated. And it is not always cultivated in youth sport. Research actually shows us that the longer one plays sport, the less likely one will engage in ethical behavior.[6] The harsh reality is that the way sport is configured in most places, it may just as likely teach children to cheat, bend the rules, and see what they can get away with much more than demonstrating ethical, socially responsible or caring behaviors.

There is a second assumption that many in the youth sports world make that further undermines the ability of youth sports to deliver character outcomes. This is the idea that the professional model of sports is appropriate for youth. More often than not, we mirror our youth sports programs after the professional model without exploring the implications of doing so. For example, hosting a national championship tournament for 7- to 9-year-old football players ignores much of what the world of child development says about what this age group needs. And that is before we consider the safety implications of extending a contact-filled football season for children with still-developing brains.

When our youth sports programs follow the professional model, it's easy to understand why parents and coaches over-emphasize performance and winning. In many cases, these characteristics have led parents to have wildly unrealistic hopes for their children. Rohloff et al. (2006) found that out of 376 parents interviewed in their study, the expectations of many parents included their children playing the sport competitively as adults.[7] Astonishingly 10% of the parents thought their child would play professionally! And over a third expected that their child would play in college. In reality, in almost all sports fewer than 2% will ever compete professionally. And depending on the sport, the chances of going from high school to the NCAA varies from 3.3% to 11.3%.[8] And yet still, parents believe that their child will earn a scholarship or become the next Tiger Woods, Serena Williams, Mia Hamm, Tom Brady or LeBron James.

We also know that many of these stories are cautionary tales about the emotional cost of driving children too hard, too soon. Ogilvie et al. (1998) called this phenomenon, "Achievement by Proxy Distortion" (ABPD).[9] The main indicators of whether parents' aspirations have become distorted can be characterized as, "the child is seen as an economic asset, the parent-child relationship is seen as exploitative, there is an imbalance to other family members' needs, and the imbalance is also exhibited at the community level as parents become adversarial, migratory, and dependent on child performance."

The way our youth sports system is structured points not towards the character development that we want, but instead incubates some of the characteristics

38 Why Change the Game?

of sport that are potentially damaging. A youth sports system that values character development would be structured around age-appropriate tasks and would take into account the right time and ways for youth to learn the valuable lessons that sport has to offer: e.g., how to compete, how to work as a team, and how to keep doing things even when they are hard.

Expectations for Interest and Fun

Many parents assume that their kids *want* to play sport and will enjoy their experience in it. They sign up their kids and do the work of getting them to practice and games in the expectation that their kids will enjoy the experience. Yet often, this expectation is not met.

First, after initial exposure experiences like tee-ball, biddy soccer and mite hockey, many youth sport settings are organized around *ability*, not *participation*. The adults running sport leagues often are *not* focused upon trying to deliver activities that would be most engaging to the participants. Rather, the premise of organized youth sport leagues, mirroring professional sport, is increasingly about determining who is "the best." Too many youth sports coaches spend more time "drafting" teams, selecting all-star teams or determining who should make the "select," "travel" or "elite" team than figuring out how all the kids might thrive and enjoy their sport regardless of ability. Even at the youngest levels, kids have to "earn" their participation. The unconfident or socially vulnerable child is particularly susceptible to an adult telling them they might not be good enough. Many teams are coached by parents that really struggle to be objective about their own child's ability. Stories are legion about the coaches' sons or daughters getting nearly all the meaningful playing opportunities to improve, at the expense of others. During this process many kids lose interest and drop out.

Second, there are increasingly many other opportunities to have fun, to be engaged in interesting activity *outside* of sport. Chief among these is the very new influence in our children's lives mentioned above: video games. Whether on a computer, a handheld device, or a console, we have all seen kids riveted for hours, playing electronic games alone, for far longer than they usually play physical games. We are not the first to wonder about the impact this is having on kids' participation in what we may now have to call face-to-face games! Formalized sport leagues and programs for children are losing ground to videogames because face-to-face sports no longer seem to be designed with a child's brain in mind.

Long before video games existed on our cell phones, kids sought to entertain themselves. Healthy children have always sought to challenge themselves and stretch their abilities. Children used to do things like climb trees, see how many times in a row they could jump over a rope, or see how many times they could skip a rock across a pond. Adults have channeled the natural disposition to be challenged into more formal and organized forms of play that fall under the category of youth sport. As youth sport has becomes increasingly organized and "serious," for many kids it may have lost its intrinsic value.

Nowadays, it is more difficult for children to be the masters of their own experience: parents sign their child up for sport, pay the fees, drive them there, and coach them officially or unofficially. Parents believe they are doing the best for their children, but if a child is conscripted into youth sport and feels compelled to stay with it because their parents paid a lot for the opportunity, what sort of impact do those things have on voluntary engagement and children experiencing the sheer joy of autonomy?

Expectations That the Competition Brings Out the Best in Us

Many parents expect that when their child engages in a competition, win or lose, the impact will be positive. There is much to learn from winning *and* from losing. But yet it is common to see on game day that the competition gives rise to a lot of behaviors that don't promote learning. Most violent acts and other egregious behaviors of adults and players happen surrounding a game. The crazy stuff we all see in the news is taking place because of the emotionally charged atmosphere that comes with "game day."

In some leagues the strategy to defuse the angst around games is to de-emphasize the score, but that rarely works. John coached his daughter's recreation basketball team in a league where they do *not* keep score. Despite this, the girls on the team, some of whom still did not know what double-dribbling was, seemed to all know and keep track of the score. In fact, one player brought her own little notebook to make sure she kept the score. Regardless of whether the score is public or not, competition seems to fire up emotions around the games.

The reality is that on game day, in so many leagues across the country, what is lurking right on the sidelines are parental aggressions, coach pettiness, parent-fueled player selfishness, fans losing all common sense and countless other human misunderstandings. These can add up to a bad scene that tears down the purpose of the whole enterprise. The expectation that competition brings out the best in us is not realized. The opportunity to leverage what is good about competition—the amped-up excitement, the opportunity to practice skills in a context that matters, and the joy of testing one team's skills against another team's—is left unfulfilled.

Current Approaches and Their Limitations

The primary reason we have created this book is not to deconstruct all that is wrong with youth sport. In fact, it's just the opposite. We want to contribute some solutions, based on the approach we describe in Chapters 1 and 2. We have offered these problematic examples to demonstrate where we are falling short

40 Why Change the Game?

in delivering for youth the experience we want them to have in sport—one that prioritizes safety, fitness, the development of character and fun. Part of this shortcoming has to do with the limitations of current approaches to managing the youth sports environment.

Fortunately, there are many places where the negative trends we discussed above are being actively challenged. Long before we began to work on Sport System Re-Design, many people have tried to reverse the negative outcomes we described. In the past two decades there has been significant growth in the number of youth-centered programs that utilize sport as a way to achieve positive outcomes, on and off the field. Coaches, league administrators, program directors and others are exploring how to create a sporting experience that maximizes the positive impact on players, both in the sporting arena and in life beyond it. The emergence of exciting new ways of leveraging sport comes at a time when highly publicized negative incidents in sport are becoming increasingly common. It appears the time has come for a "fundamental rethink" (Jones, 2010) in the way we conceptualize sport. When sport "works," it seamlessly delivers physical, emotional and psychological benefits. Because it is what has been called "an embodied experience,"[10] it has the power to be transformational.

As we mentioned in Chapter 1, when a league administrator, coach, parent or volunteer commits to trying to deliver these great outcomes, they often employ one of two strategies to influence the quality of the sports environment. They focus on coach education, or they create a curriculum.

1. **Coach Education**: This includes all the ways that coaches are trained informally and formally, as well as the information that is provided to coaches about how to improve their own "practice." This information is typically about what they "know" and what they must be able to "do."
2. **Curriculum**: This includes the activities, instructional strategies and learning expectations that a coach is attempting to deliver over the course of their season. The curriculum typically dictates the goals of a practice and what a coach does to achieve those goals.

There is no doubt that coaches play an influential role in the player's experience and can help drive the outcomes that we all want youth to achieve through sports. Educating coaches on principles of youth development can help them see what is and isn't appropriate for youth of different ages or backgrounds. Coach education that focuses on effective instruction techniques can help young players build their sports skills in a way that develops their efficacy: they go from thinking that they can't do something to believing that they can. Helping coaches employ strategies to encourage players to take every opportunity to practice making good decisions and taking ownership over their behavior can sometimes turn a kid who is too shy to contribute into a team leader. Coach education that

Why Change the Game? **41**

does these things can certainly help move the needle when it comes to what most would consider universally desired outcomes.

There are, however, some realities in youth sport that limit the impact that coach education can have on the sports environment. First is the limitation of *time*. Youth sports is an industry powered by volunteers, many of them working parents, for whom time is at a premium. Coaches, who are usually volunteers, thus have limited time for training. So naturally, spending time at training can be a low priority for many. When John was in the middle of giving a talk about youth development to a Little League group of about 20 parents who were also coaches, one of the parents raised his hand and commented to the group, "This stuff you are talking about and having us think about is really great, but the guys who need to hear this are not here." In other words, the people who show up to the kinds of coach education available for youth sport often are not those who need it most.

Second is the limitation of *expertise*. Most coaches and staff of youth sports organizations chose to be involved because they loved their sport, not because they have a background in youth development, education, social work or even coaching. There are not nearly enough people with the right expertise to train the number of coaches who are working in youth sports.

Third is the limitation of *interpretation*. No matter how well-informed the coach education program or how many hours go into a coach's education, all of the information will still be filtered through each individual coach's experience and context. Like teaching, coaching is an applied science. That is to say, there are some knowledgeable people that do not make good coaches. And there are others that are not so knowledgeable who get the best out of their players. This centers around the divide of the "science of coaching," which is the technical and tactical knowledge of sport, and the "art of coaching," which has more to do with the communication, psychology and motivational parts of coaching. Therefore, no matter how much knowledge you provide to a coach, you may not be able to give that coach the skills and abilities that are also necessary to be an effective coach. Individual differences in behavior and approach will always mean that coach education is internalized and implemented differently with different coaches.

Programs that want to be more intentional about the experience that kids are having can also look to curriculum for answers. A good curriculum provides structure and consistency to a team. When delivered in the way it is intended, it highlights important messages that a program wants their participants to hear. Good curriculum provides critical questions for coaches to ask that will help young people think about the lessons they are learning in meaningful ways. But, like coach education, curriculum is also limited by the time, expertise and interpretation of the person delivering the curriculum.

Because Up2Us Sports works with so many sports-based youth development programs around the country, Megan has seen lots of really well-constructed

42 Why Change the Game?

curriculum that is intended to dictate the focus of the program. However, in practice, it rarely does. Coaches, even those who intend to administer the curriculum, often find themselves without the time (in absolute time and in prioritized time) to administer lessons that are an "add-on" to the sport's activities. Further, many of them don't have the skills or experience to deliver the lessons in the way they were intended. Every lesson, no matter how explicitly written, gets delivered through the filter of the person delivering it. They may fail to highlight crucial lessons or be challenged to explain the activity in an effective way.

These limitations make us hungry for another way to accomplish our goals of making sport a great experience for children and youth. They make us want to add something to the arsenal that sets more coaches and sports environments up for success. If we want to change the youth sports environment for the better, we need more than just coach education and curriculum. We need a third approach that fills in the gaps of human error and other limitations.

In our view, this third approach, described in Chapters 1 and 2, is Sport System Re-Design. We think it could dramatically increase the likelihood that every coach will adhere to the principles and reinforce the values the league prioritizes. This approach could help a program provide a great sports experience for every kid, every time. It can get us the outcomes we seek through youth sports—kids who are active, have fun, develop character and grow as an athletes.

In the next chapter, we introduce some of the inspirations for this approach. We then move on to Part 2: Case Studies and Part 3: the Sport System Re-Design Toolkit.

Notes

1. MLBcommunity.org. (n.d.). Retrieved April 27, 2015, from http://web.mlbcommunity.org/programs/rbi.jsp?content=history.
2. Has Baseball's Moment Passed? *Wall Street Journal*, March 31, 2011. http://online.wsj.com/article/SB10001424052748703712504576232753156582750.html retrieved 1/2/13.
3. Steinberg, L. (2014, September 4). Why the NFL is America's passion. Retrieved April 27, 2015, from www.forbes.com/sites/leighsteinberg/2014/09/04/why-the-nfl-is-americas-passion/.
4. Let's Move. (n.d.). Retrieved April 27, 2015, from www.letsmove.gov/learn-facts/epidemic-childhood-obesity.
5. Woods, R. (2011). Social issues in sport. Champaign, IL: Human Kinetics.
6. Long, T., Pantaléon, N., & Bruant, G. (2008, December) Institutionalization versus self regulation: a contextual analysis of responsibility among adolescent sportsmen. *Journal of Moral Education 37*(4), 519–538.
7. Rohloff, R., Frea, A. G., Busey, S. L., Dempsey, R. L., & Young, C. C. (2006). Parent values for coaching practices and discipline in youth sports. *Medicine and Science in Sports and Exercise, 38*(5), Supplement abstract 1741.
8. Probability of competing beyond high school. (2013, December 17). Retrieved April 27, 2015, from www.ncaa.org/about/resources/research/probability-competing-beyond-high-school.

9. Ogilvie, B. C., Tofler, I. R., Conroy, D. E., & Drell, M. J. (1998). Comprehending role conflicts in the coaching of children, adolescents, and young adults. Transference, countertransference, and achievement by proxy distortion paradigms. *Child and Adolescent Psychiatric Clinics of North America, 7*(4), 879–890.
10. Agans, J. P., Säfvenbom, R., Davis, J. L., Bowers, E. P., & Lerner, R. M. (2013). Positive movement experiences: Approaching the study of athletic participation, exercise, and leisure activity through relational developmental systems theory and the concept of embodiment. *Advances in Child Development and Behavior, 45*, 261–286.

References

Agans, J. P., Säfvenbom, R., Davis, J. L., Bowers, E. P., & Lerner, R. M. (2013). Positive movement experiences: Approaching the study of athletic participation, exercise, and leisure activity through relational developmental systems theory and the concept of embodiment. *Advances in Child Development and Behavior, 45*, 261–286.

Futterman, M. (2011). Has baseball's moment passed? *Wall Street Journal.* Retrieved January 2, 2013, from http://online.wsj.com/article/SB10001424052748703712504576232753156582750.html.

Jones, R. (2006). The sports coach as educator: Reconceptualising sports coaching. *International Journal of Sports Science and Coaching, 1*(4), 405–412.

Let's Move. (n.d.). Retrieved April 27, 2015, from www.letsmove.gov/learn-facts/epidemic-childhood-obesity.

Long, T., Pantaléon, N., & Bruant, G. (2008). Institutionalization versus self-regulation: A contextual analysis of responsibility among adolescent Sportsmen. *Journal of Moral Education, 37*(4), 519–538.

MLBcommunity.org. (n.d.). Retrieved April 27, 2015, from http://web.mlbcommunity.org/programs/rbi.jsp?content=history.

Ogilvie, B. C., Tofler, I. R., Conroy, D. E., & Drell, M. J. (1998). Comprehending role conflicts in the coaching of children, adolescents, and young adults. Transference, countertransference, and achievement by proxy distortion paradigms. *Child and Adolescent Psychiatric Clinics of North America, 7*(4), 879–890.

Probability of competing beyond high school. (2013, December 17). Retrieved April 27, 2015, from www.ncaa.org/about/resources/research/probability-competing-beyond-high-school.

Rohloff, R., Frea, A. G., Busey, S. L., Dempsey, R. L., & Young, C. C. (2006). Parent values for coaching practices and discipline in youth sports. *Medicine and Science in Sports and Exercise, 38*(5), Supplement abstract 1741.

Steinberg, L. (2014, September 4). Why the NFL is America's passion. Retrieved April 27, 2015, from www.forbes.com/sites/leighsteinberg/2014/09/04/why-the-nfl-is-americas-passion/.

Woods, R. (2011). Social issues in Sport, 2nd edition eBook. Champaign, IL: Human Kinetics.

4

SOURCES OF INSPIRATION

Sport System Re-Design (SSRD) emerged from our thinking about critical experiences we have each had working in youth sport. Our convergence around SSRD coincided with each of us individually arriving at a common conclusion: Better coach education and more advanced curriculum were still falling short of the outcomes we deeply believed were possible inside the sport programs we were studying, consulting with and working in. Time and time again, we would take two steps forward towards a desired outcome only to find ourselves taking one or sometimes two steps back.

We have come to realize that each of us was imprinted with the raw material for SSRD during our childhoods. Each of us was fortunate to grow up in neighborhoods in which we could experience free play and the joy of games. John, being a middle child of seven, was constantly tagging along with his older brother to every possible throwing, running and catching game in the street, against the back of a house or in a nearby parking lot or park. He also had many early experiences with mainstream team sports: football, basketball and baseball.

John got hooked on sports when his eyes were opened to the power of sport to shape a person. As the quarterback for his high school football team, John had become used to having his coach use gestures and hand signals from the sidelines to transmit the play that he was supposed to run. Until, in one particular game, his coach didn't give him the signal. Instead, when John looked to him for the play, his coach simply pointed at John. Confused, John then pointed at himself, yelling to the sideline, "You want me to call the play?" The coach nodded in agreement and made a shooing gesture and mouthed, "You got it." At first, this was a moment of extreme uncertainty for John, but he turned to his huddled teammates and stammered through calling his first play. The play worked out okay. He turned back again to his coach,

46 Sources of Inspiration

and the coach again exhorted him, "Keep going!" From that moment, instead of waiting for the coach, he started looking at the defense in an entirely different way. He experienced an unrushed feeling of control for the rest of the game and that entire series that was exhilarating.

In that moment, two things happened. First, John experienced a kind of "ownership" over the game of football that he had not previously experienced. He felt an immediate and permanent surge of confidence that he could play the game, not for someone else, but for himself. He experienced a tangible outcome that was not measured on the scoreboard. Second, he began to scrutinize the game much more closely. He marveled at the profound impact that his coach's seemingly small change in role and approach had upon him.

Indirectly, that moment led to a full-time career teaching and training coaches at Boston University. And though he has dedicated his career to providing the best coach education possible, and he has retained his close scrutiny and focus on outcomes, he has felt that something was missing, and his work was not having the impact he hoped for.

For Megan, siblings also played a significant role in her development, but so did geography. She grew up in a beach town on a dead-end street. This meant more freedom to play at home and plenty of summer days making up games in the sand. Add to the equation a twin brother and parents who firmly believed that she could do anything that he could do, and like John, she grew up with ample opportunity to hone her athletic and inventive play, even when opportunities for girls were sometimes scarce.

Megan navigated a high school and college soccer career, spent some time coaching college soccer and then found her dream job at America SCORES. What was unique about SCORES was the simple fact that they ran their own soccer leagues. With complete control over all aspects of their leagues, the coaches and program leadership would find themselves in engaging conversations and debates about their participants' athletic and personal development. She remembers their lively debates about whether to allow heading, the role of the referee as a teacher and not just an enforcer, and how to create more parity between teams.

For Lou, the roots of re-Design were nurtured with his younger brother and a handful of friends on the hardtop playground of Liberty Elementary School in Pittsburgh, PA. Looking back, a book could have been filled with the variations of tag and football that were invented and the countless rules that only the "King" of the playground game four-square could call. At age eight, Lou organized 20 classmates and convinced his fourth grade teacher to referee soccer matches on weekends. To help convince his teacher, he actually promised his father's tickets to a Pittsburgh Steelers game—unbeknownst to his father!

Throughout college and beyond, Lou found himself in a series of sports-based youth-facing jobs that etched in his mind that the real fun in sport comes from tinkering with the game until it works just right. Running "open gym" for 7- to

Sources of Inspiration **47**

17-year-olds at the Boys and Girls Club will convert anyone into a re-Designer in no time!

Then, in 2009, Lou was hired to work with Doc Wayne Youth Services (DWYS), a competitive four-sport league for adolescents affected by complex trauma, and help create a therapeutic curriculum embedded inside the league. Through observation and interviews, he quickly came to realize that a traditional curriculum would not suffice, and that there were a wide range of tweaks and changes to the sport itself that would fuel the key outcomes that the league desired to achieve for this special population.

Our stories likely mirror many of yours. In fact, as you'll see later in this chapter, most of us make it to adulthood with some level of learned wiring for re-Design. The unfortunate reality is that somewhere between claiming our first victory in "four-square," "running bases" or any other games we played in childhood, and our involvement in more traditional forms of organized competitive sport, many of us have lost our comfort with or the inclination to re-Design our games.

Yet, the spirit of re-Design is still there. At every SSRD conference we've hosted, we have seen everyone in the room awaken to the possibility of re-Design by tapping into their inventive and childlike nature. With a framework and process, we believe you'll be able to do the same. You will find your own source of inspiration to look at your sport with closer scrutiny. And we hope in a similar way, you'll start to think about re-Design as part of the answer to the question, "What isn't working in my youth sport program?"

After all, games are simply social constructions. That is to say, just like most of us did as children, we can agree to change the rules of engagement at any point to make a game better. But the longer we have been influenced by the organized and formal structure of sport, the more we think that games are a fixed entity. In this book we hope more people find encouragement and full permission to change their game.

This chapter will introduce you to eight formal sources of inspiration for re-Design. As we have formalized SSRD, we've looked far and wide, inside and outside of sport, for ways in which people are using the concept of design and re-Design to achieve incredible outcomes. Each of these sources holds some of the DNA of SSRD and has fueled our collective thinking and inventing around maximizing the impact of youth sport.

Source #1: Systems Thinking

As we briefly described in the Preface, one of our first insights that eventually led to Sport System Re-Design was the realization that sport itself is a system. While sport sociologists have examined social issues and controversies from a systemic viewpoint for some time, framing sport as a system led us directly to the field of systems theory and systems thinking. In systems thinking, we study a "thing" in relation to that thing's interaction with other parts of a system.

48 Sources of Inspiration

Systems thinking promotes looking at problems from an expansive view and taking into account the interactions that happen between parts of the system. This allows for a fuller examination of what drives human behavior, which usually results in more focused and integrated solutions. It encourages the question, "Why is something happening?" and urges us to keep asking these kind of questions until we find better answers. In human systems, quite often the best answers are not always obvious. To discover subtle but elegant solutions, we must expand the range of possibilities we usually consider.

For example, climate scientists find it necessary to use systems thinking in order to gain an understanding of the environment and how we can protect it for future generations. If we were only to focus on the polar ice caps melting and seek the answer to that problem outside of the complex and dynamic ecosystems in which they reside, we would not be able to uncover the deeper sources and possible solutions for that issue that rest far away from the ice caps themselves.

The theory and practice of systems thinking help us see youth sport through a broader lens. When looking through that lens, we begin to see certain aspects of sport that play a significant role in the young person's sport experience. But we also find that these elements are neglected or under-emphasized in favor of what appears, on the surface, to be the most important elements—coaches, for example. This approach forces us to consider that coach training might not be the only or even the best means to achieve a desired outcome.

Systems thinking challenges practitioners to focus on *high leverage points* in any system. These are the parts of the system that have the potential to have a disproportionate amount of impact relative to the input required to move that part of the system. The marine trim tab is the classic example of a high point of

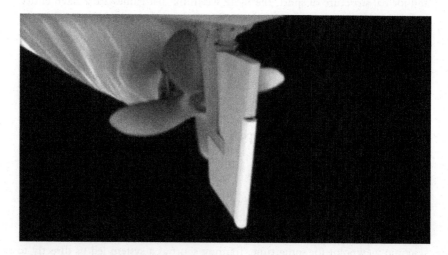

FIGURE 4.1 Systems Thinking: Trim Tab

Credit: Blondie Hasler / Wikimedia Commons

leverage. A trim tab is a small bendable flap that fits into a boat's rudder. The trim tab, though tiny compared to the size of a boat, has a dramatic impact on a boat's ability to turn. In other words, small change = big impact.

The concept of high leverage is vital to systems thinking and therefore to Sport System Re-Design. When we look at any sport system, we look to uncover high leverage points that we can change that will have a significant impact. If enough practitioners work in a similar fashion, there is the potential to transform even the entire sport system itself.

Source #2: Behavioral Economics

SSRD draws heavily from emerging trends and current research in promoting behavior change. Several current behavior change theories, including behavioral economics, explore ways that large and often subtle changes to the environment can effectuate change.

Behavioral economics is a field that looks at the ways we can change the environment and the structure of important choices, habits and actions, in order to influence our behavior. Instead of looking at will or motivation, or even curriculum, behavioral economists seek to find ways to understand or shift behavior by examining factors in the environment, in the surroundings of a person. One of the terms for this is "choice architecture." It is most commonly used to describe the many different ways that choices can be presented to consumers and the impact that the presentation has on decision-making.

This term can be applied to any situation in which the way a choice is presented can influence the decision. For example, Laura Smith, researcher at Cornell's Food and Brand Lab (Smith, Just, & Wansink, 2010), experimented with changes to the environment to increase salad consumption at a high school. She discovered that by moving the salad bar four feet closer to the cash registers, there was a 250–300% increase in salad consumption. Moving the salad bar to a new location "made it easier for them (the students) to make the right choice." Google, among other organizations, has conducted similar experiments in their employee cafeteria.

One of the most profound examples of behavioral economics involves the dramatic shift of participants in organ donation programs in the U.S. in the past 20 years (Richard, 2009). Typically, when a person registers for their driver's license, they are asked to opt-in for the national organ donor program. Despite large-scale public service campaigns and surveys that indicated that most Americans would agree to be donors, the percentages have always been very low. After close examination of the system, the choice on the driver's license form to opt-in to donate organs was changed to an opt-out. Organ donor registry rates are now around 82% (Johnson & Goldstein, 2003).

Behavioral economics has helped us look more closely at the structures of sport and the influence they have on behavior. In particular, what we draw from

FIGURE 4.2 Behavior Economics: Child in Line at Salad Bar
Credit: Steve Debenport / iStock

behavioral economics is that by thoughtfully tinkering with the "design" of sport, we can nudge people towards or away from certain behaviors. Behavior economics gives us permission to change what is in the environment of sport in order to change behavior.

Source #3: Adapted Sports

One of the most important sources for SSRD is actually inside the world of sport itself. If we turn our attention towards the world of adapted sport, we discover some of the most creative and game-changing re-Designs, all in support of creating more access for more people to play.

Adapted sport has a rich history that goes back many decades. Practitioners in this field can speak firsthand about the many creative and powerful ways in which they have tweaked and re-Designed various sports to accommodate participants with physical, intellectual or emotional challenges. Consider:

1. **Sled Hockey**: This was one of the breakout sports of the 2014 Winter Olympics, which allows for amputees and paraplegics to sit in a fitted seat-sled to skate on ice. Using two mini-sticks, one held in each hand, which double as propulsion devices, teams of six compete.
2. **Quad Rugby**: Popularized in the 2005 movie "Murderball," quad rugby centers around a specially designed wheelchair that can sustain the type of contact expected in rugby, adapted to play on a gymnasium surface.

3. **Sitting Volleyball**: This is a version of volleyball that maintains the fast pace, exciting rallies and team dynamics of traditional volleyball. There are a host of rules to sitting volleyball, but at the center is a net that is approximately three feet high with team members sitting instead of standing. It's a brilliantly simple adaptation that has created tremendous access to a sport that otherwise would be near impossible to play by anyone with a lower body disability.

Something remarkable happens to our creativity and ability to re-Design when we embrace the challenge of adapting a sport for a person or population who could not otherwise participate. Assumptions about what is sacred or not sacred in the game are dropped for the cause of access. Instead, we put every aspect of the game on the table to make the sport work for a specific population.

Once these assumptions about what we can and can't do in sport are dropped, incredible innovations take shape. Consider Beep Baseball. Beep Baseball is a remarkable example of an adapted sport that has succeeded in creating access for partial and completely blind players to play baseball. The re-Designs in Beep Baseball are comprehensive by necessity. The ball includes a mechanism that causes it to beep, thus allowing any player to track it without sight. The bases are inflatable pylons (which also beep!). These allow a player to run full speed towards the base, despite not being able to see. There is a complete rule book that rivals that of sighted baseball, covering everything from strikes to innings to at-bats.

FIGURE 4.3 Adapted Sports: Sled Hockey

Credit: Jason V / iStock

FIGURE 4.4 Adapted Sports: Quad Rugby

Credit: Rob van Esch / Shutterstock

FIGURE 4.5 Adapted Sports: Sitting Volleyball

Credit: Pukhov Konstantin / Shutterstock

Beep Baseball is a wonderful example of a sport where there have been changes in all aspects of the sport: the equipment, the playing space, the rules of the game and the roles that people play. Beep Baseball even includes adaptations to the roles the fans play. In order to allow everyone to hear the ball, spectators of Beep Baseball must remain silent during pitches and hits.

Special Olympics, which aspires to create sport opportunities for players with intellectual disabilities, has been re-designing the traditional model of sport through their "Unified Sport" approach.[1] Instead of creating versions of sport that a certain population can separately play, they are reinventing the rules and roles of many popular sports, like soccer, track and field, ice skating, and snowboarding, so that players with and without intellectual disabilities can play together.

Adapted sports help us see what is possible inside sport when we no longer hold the way a sport is played as sacred, but instead allow ourselves to look at sport through the lens of a *desired outcome*. Adapted Sport practitioners have a distinct focus: how to re-Design a sport to allow for the most access possible for a population that otherwise could not access that sport.

Source #4: Universal Design

Universal design attempts to create environments and products that allow for the most use by the widest range of people possible. Universal design aspires to shatter barriers to access by creating things that are "usable" without the need for specialized adaptation or design for a certain population. Universal designers seek fully integrated solutions that take all users into account from the start.

Historically, we have adapted products and environments for certain populations only after we have created a solution for a majority population, typically an able-bodied audience. In contrast, Universal designers start their work trying to answer the question: "What would a solution look like that could work for everyone?" This question provokes a much broader and more creative way of thinking, resulting in solutions that are highly accessible and promote integration of people who might otherwise be segregated for physical, cognitive and other reasons. Moreover, the designs are often elegant and visually stunning.

Universal design pushes the spectrum of access to an entirely new level. Instead of accepting a ramp alongside a set of steps, universal design poses the question: "Could the two be seamlessly integrated, thus allowing for people of all abilities to travel together?" The image on the next page is a stunning example of this kind of integrated design.

Consider the typical kitchen and the standard appliances that are used in that space. They are all designed for someone who can stand and who can lean in and over and thus, safely navigate their way through preparing a meal. A universal

54 Sources of Inspiration

FIGURE 4.6 Universal Design: Stair/Ramp

Credit: "UBC Continuing Studies," permission by Cheyenne Parizeau, University of British Columbia

designer looks at a kitchen and wonders not just how to make it accessible to someone in a wheelchair, but ponders how to engineer a stove, for example, that would be fully accessible for both someone in a wheelchair and someone standing.

The practice of Universal Design inspires a profound new take on the "stove top," functional, usable and beautiful. This is a similar approach to the Unified Sport approach of Special Olympics, in which "normal" athletes and those with "intellectual disabilities" can take to the court, field or track together.

As with adapted sport, universal design inspires us to see everything around us and wonder how it can best be constructed to work for everyone in a flexible, equitable and intuitive way. It fuels "design thinking" and challenges us to accept nothing as sacred or unchangeable. It reminds us that the way we work, play and live is just a current iteration and that if we choose to, we can reimagine and reinvent everything we use into something better.

Universal design fuels our thinking about SSRD. It insists on elevating our outcomes to be more inviting, more inclusive and more accessible for more people. For many of us, these are the types of outcomes we aspire to achieve in our sport programs.

FIGURE 4.7 Universal Design: Stove

Credit: Barrier Free Architecturals Inc. www.barrierfree.org

56 Sources of Inspiration

Source #5: The History of Professional and Collegiate Sport

One of the most important and surprising inspirations of SSRD comes from the hallowed stadiums of our most popular professional and college sports.

For many players, coaches and fans, the idea of changing any aspect of *their* sport, especially at the college or pro-level, is unimaginable. The "way" we play our sport is sacred. However, history reveals to us that just about every professional and college sport played today has been and continues to be re-Designed.

Every year, presidents, administrators, experts and coaches from your favorite sport will convene, usually during the off-season, to consider changes to the sport. At some point before the next season, they will announce the official changes. Re-Design is all around us in the sports that we cherish and can't imagine ever changing.

In the appendix of this book, we've documented some of the hundreds of re-Designs that professional sports have undergone over the past century.

Recall the example we introduced in Chapter 1: the sport of basketball. Basketball, a sport invented by James Naismith in 1891, has one of the most profound track records of re-Design. First created as a form of winter conditioning for athletes in Springfield, MA, it has gone through tremendous re-Design and evolution over the past 100+ years. The backboard was not introduced until 1893, the "jump ball" in 1936 and the 24-second shot clock (for the NBA) in 1954. Since then, the NBA has introduced the 3-point shot, taken it out of the game and put it back in.

If we examine just about every sport that is played professionally or at the college level, we will find that the sport as we currently know it is not the sport that it was in the past. People have been changing and adapting sport for a long time for many reasons:

- **A desire for a different outcome in the sport**: Soccer has explored re-Designing for more goals. Hockey has re-Designed for fewer games that end in a tie. Softball has instituted the "mercy rule" to end a game if it becomes too lopsided.
- **The need to use technology to enhance judgment of referees and umpires**: Football instituted "instant replay" and equipped coaches and referees with the tools and rules to utilize it effectively. Soccer has recently instituted "goal line technology" to verify goals scored.
- **Demand from spectators and players for a "better game"**: Salary caps in many professional sports have helped create more parity of play between more teams. Basketball's shot clock has helped speed up the game, promoting more shooting and scoring, which enhances the experience for spectators.
- **Public pressure for increased safety**: From the professional to the youth level, millions of dollars are being invested in technology and other means

to reduce, and hopefully eliminate, concussions and traumatic brain injury while preserving other core elements of the game. These efforts represent one of the most public and most profound examples of SSRD. This has implications for the entire sport as well as for other games like hockey, lacrosse and soccer in which there is a high incidence of concussion.

Professional and collegiate sports are an important source of inspiration for SSRD. Knowing that the governing bodies of these leagues and associations are constantly tinkering with their sport reminds us that SSRD is and always has been part of sport, even at the highest levels of play in our society. This also is a vital reminder that no matter how sacred and unchangeable we think it is, people throughout history have worked intentionally to change sport and will likely continue to do so in the future.

Source #6: The Playground

Most of us spent time during our childhood playing active games. We ran, chased and tagged. We circled bases. We bounced and threw balls and before adults got heavily involved, we likely invented our own games. We find that when pressed to reflect, most adults tell us about a game that they and some of their friends and family invented. Often, these games are incredibly sophisticated with long lists of rules and specific roles for people to play. For example, an invented game that one of us used to play was "Off the Wall." Any number of players would throw a "pinkie" or tennis ball off a wall, and everyone would try to catch that ball. As players eventually dropped these highly contested catches, the offending players that had accumulated three drops would then have to run along the wall between two points, and the "winner" could throw the ball at the players until they made a predetermined number of back and forth trips, allowing them to get back in the game.

Children, when left to their own devices, will twist and bend even well-known games to meet their needs. Four-square is a game that on the surface is very simple: bounce and hit the ball into one another's square and try to advance to the top of four spots on the square. Yet, the game of four-square has evolved dozens and dozens of times through rules and variations. The child in the top spot on the square can implement any of these rules to make the game more or less competitive and more or less fair for those playing. It is one of the greatest natural examples of Sport System Re-Design in action; all controlled by whichever child reigns champion.

We believe that re-Design comes naturally to us all. It is wired into us as children. Very small children are the best at creating games that fit the context they are in. In the process of "growing up" and getting involved in organized sports, children cede this control to adults. Any change to our sport is decided by the league administrators and governing bodies, not the participants.

FIGURE 4.8 Playground: 4 Square
Credit: Up2Us Sports

We know how our sport is played and therefore, by default, are potential re-Design experts. However, we must remember that the playground is in all of us. We can allow ourselves to revisit the feeling and the freedom of inventing a game or of re-inventing a sport, the way children would if given permission. Then we can channel this source of inspiration to fuel our search for the outcomes we want to achieve through sport.

Source #7: The History of Breakthrough Inventions

The history of the world is one of re-Design. For every invention—the creation of something new—there usually follows tens, hundreds and even thousands of re-Designs. We can trace the journey of any modern device and find a series of fascinating re-Designs. Some of those re-Designs are substantial, and some are just tiny tweaks. Regardless, we need only look around our homes to see the art of re-Design permeating our lives.

Consider how we watch our favorite TV shows. We can begin with the first photographs and picture shows, and follow their story as they evolved into the first motion pictures and eventually to the first television sets. Our current experience of watching "content" through our portable devices and on instant demand has gone through many re-Designs since the first television sets were sold less than 100 years ago.

Each of these innovations represents a re-Design. Some person, team or company decided to take a closer look at what we were currently using and put their brain power and resources towards trying whatever they could to make it better. These true inventors constantly ask questions such as "Why not?" and "What if . . .?" They are not satisfied with the status quo and see every element of a product as something that can be modified, tweaked and changed for the better.

One of our favorite inventions is the SOCCKET. It also happens to be a sports-based re-Design so we like it even more! SOCCKET is the invention of two undergraduate students from Harvard University. Tasked with using a multi-player game to tackle a social issue, they searched for ways to economically provide more light to people in developing countries, without expensive electricity infrastructure.

These young innovators took the mechanism that allows someone to shake a flashlight to produce hand-generated electricity and engineered a way to embed that type of mechanism inside a soccer ball. The result is that the act of dribbling the ball, as you would in any game, will produce enough electricity to power a small attachable lamp. One hour of play can produce up to three hours of light!

The SOCCKET is a truly brilliant re-Design. It harnesses people's interest in playing soccer and combines it with technology that would propel that interest into a real, practical solution. When we hear about these kinds of re-Designs, we find ourselves also wondering, **why not**? Why can't we change the way we organize youth sports? Why does the game have to be played the way it has been historically? What would happen if we did make a change, or two, or twelve?

Inventors remind us that the world as we know it was built by people who imagined new and better ways to live. They inspire us to not accept things the way they are, but to believe that there is always a way to make them better.

FIGURE 4.9 Innovation: SOCCKET

Credit: SOCCKET

Source #8: Video Game Design

There is no question that video games are pervasive. It is estimated that we spend 3 billion hours a week as a planet playing video games.[2] Almost 200 million people in the US play at least one hour a day. According to Jane McGonigal, author of the 2011 book, *Reality Is Broken: Why Games Make Us Better and How They Can Change the World Now,* "The younger you are, the more likely you are to be a gamer." McGonigal's data reveals that the average young person plays 10,000 hours of video games by the age of twenty-one.

There are many reasons for the incredible allure of video games. For SSRD, we are particularly interested in the close attention video game designers have paid to what people—particularly children and young people—want from their experience.

John's 11-year-old son, Luke, is a particularly precocious cyber-citizen who actually studies this stuff. When asked what he likes about videogames, his first response was, "You get to customize it to your own liking. You can add characters that have 'special powers' to the game . . . You can pick the type of arena that you battle in or the type of weapons you use or the name and shape of your character." Luke's explanation illustrates how the ability to control the game is part of the draw for him.

Research on human psychology has shown that the intense draw of video games includes:[3,4]

- Meeting a need for control.
- Measures of one's progress in tight feedback loops.

FIGURE 4.10 Video Games: Group of Children Playing
Credit: SerrNovik / iStock

- Fostering of relationships with friends.
- Opportunities to invent and create elements of the game.
- Varied and increasing levels of challenge; and setting individual conditions for level of challenge.

For video game designers, their outcome is game play, and they have, through research in human psychology and behavior, drawn out a number of powerful "hooks," which keep participants engaged. Like these video game designers, SSRD practitioners need to focus on the outcome and design for our games. We need to understand what is compelling to kids in order to make sure that we keep them interested in the game. Electronic game designers have mastered the skill of designing for an outcome and remind us to ask the question: What if we re-Designed the game itself to connect to the needs and wants of the user?

Summary

In this chapter we've described eight primary sources of inspiration for Sport System Re-Design:

1. Systems Thinking
2. Behavioral Economics
3. Adapted Sports
4. Universal Design
5. The History of Professional and Collegiate Sport
6. The Playground
7. The History of Breakthrough Inventions
8. Video Game Design

A combination of these ways of thinking gives us a rich and creative set of tools for making change. This chapter introduced these significant bodies of work and research to help drive our thinking about SSRD going forward. We hope they will provide a spark of inspiration so that we can start looking differently at our sports. When we reach across various disciplines, we open up our thinking and expand what's possible, instead of limiting it. Borrowing the best elements of these diverse fields can help us find the change we seek: that youth sports are delivered in a way that achieves maximum positive impact on youth.

Notes

1. Unified Sports. (n.d.). Retrieved April 27, 2015, from www.specialolympics.org/uni fied-sports.aspx.
2. McGonigal, J. (n.d.). We spend 3 billion hours a week as a planet playing videogames. Is it worth it? How could it be MORE worth it? | A conversation on TED.com. Retrieved April 27, 2015, from www.ted.com/conversations/44/we_spend_3_billion_ hours_a_wee.html.

62 Sources of Inspiration

3. What makes video games addictive? (2014, February 18). Retrieved April 27, 2015, from www.economist.com/blogs/babbage/2014/02/electronic-entertainment.
4. Video Game Addiction. (n.d.). Retrieved April 27, 2015, from www.video-game-addiction.org/what-makes-games-addictive.html.

References

Johnson, E. J., & Goldstein, D. G. (2003). Do defaults save lives? *Science, 302*, 1338–1339.

McGonigal, J. (n.d.). We spend 3 billion hours a week as a planet playing videogames. Is it worth it? How could it be MORE worth it? A conversation on TED.com. Retrieved April 27, 2015, from www.ted.com/conversations/44/we_spend_3_billion_hours_a_wee.html.

McGonigal, J. (2011). *Reality is broken: Why games make us better and how they can change the world* (New ed.). New York: Penguin Press.

Richard, T. (2009, September 26). Opting in vs. opting out. *The New York Times.* Retrieved April 27, 2015, from www.nytimes.com/2009/09/27/business/economy/27view.html?_r=0.

Smith, L. E., Just, D. R., & Wansink, B. (2010). Convenience drives choice in school lunch rooms: A salad bar success story. *The FASEB Journal.* Retrieved April 27, 2015, from www.fasebj.org/cgi/content/meeting_abstract/24/1_MeetingAbstracts/732.11.

Unified Sports. (n.d.). Retrieved April 27, 2015, from www.specialolympics.org/unified-sports.aspx.

Video Game Addiction. (n.d.). Retrieved April 27, 2015, from www.video-game-addiction.org/what-makes-games-addictive.html.

What makes video games addictive? (2014, February 18). Retrieved April 27, 2015, from www.economist.com/blogs/babbage/2014/02/electronic-entertainment.

5

CASE STUDIES

The best way to understand the power and potential of Sport System Re-Design is to hear a story of where it's worked. It's easy to confuse the concept with better coach education or curriculum changes until we understand the often simple, yet profound, changes to the *actual game* that achieve the outcomes we've been searching for. And the idea of changing our games seems at the same time easy and unimaginable until we get to know the people who have done it.

In this section, we'll introduce you to some of the best stories we've heard in the years that we've been studying SSRD. At the heart of these stories is often the work of an innovator or small team of innovators who push to get people beyond what is comfortable or "traditional," in order to get the best possible outcome for their sport. The stories take place at different levels of sport, both professional and youth. They involve different kinds of sports: individual sports and team sports, sports that are new to a community and those that are well-established. The re-Designs in these case studies point at different kinds of outcomes, but have in common one important goal. Like many of the examples we've already outlined, these case studies start with the idea that "we can do better for our participants."

Magic Bus

They were finally outside, under open skies. Girls who wouldn't even think about having a life outside the home were running, kicking, and most importantly, laughing. Standing on the sidelines (and sometimes running alongside them) were their mothers, women who hadn't ever had a chance to play in their lives.

64 Case Studies

FIGURE 5.1 Magic Bus
Credit: Magic Bus India Foundation

Working in the urban slums of Mumbai, Magic Bus was one of the first organizations in Asia to use activities and sport as a tool for holistic community development. One of the four pillars of impact was gender equality, and convincing girls and their families to participate in group activities with boys was an uphill battle.

The Magic Bus team knew that to get more Indian girls out of their homes, they had to fight centuries of expectations, cultural norms and customs that said that the world outside the home (including playing soccer) was for boys—and that cooking and cleaning was for girls. It was going to take more than just asking to get them to take part. Before a girl could show up to a Magic Bus session, it would take a lot of convincing of a lot of people in the families and communities.

At first, the Magic Bus team thought that they would have to get the fathers to agree. In a patriarchal society, it made sense to assume that the fathers would dictate their daughters' activities. But, after having countless conversations at the homes of the girls they were recruiting for the program, Magic Bus learned something that changed their approach. They learned that it was, in fact, the mothers and grandmothers who had the most influence in how the girls spent their time. Women are the proud caretakers of a family's culture, honor and history. Mothers and grandmothers would need to be convinced that something that they had never been allowed to do was a safe and appropriate option for their daughters.

Even after they switched their focus from fathers to mothers and grandmothers, they were still not getting very far with their approach. Mothers and grandmothers were not swayed by the pleas of their daughters or the explanations of the Magic Bus staff. So they changed their tactics. They didn't ask mothers and grandmothers to let their daughters and granddaughters come out of the homes to explore a world of empowerment. They asked them to play themselves. What better way to be convinced of the physical and emotional merits of group activities than to actually get out and play themselves?

Most mothers said no. But for those mothers who showed even the slightest bit of interest, the Magic Bus team put on the full-court press. They planned pick-up games and tried to get mothers to come with their friends, so they wouldn't be alone. They could try it out for themselves and see what fun it was. Before you knew it, the mothers and grandmothers demanded a tournament of their own. All of a sudden, the same women that thought girls shouldn't even get out of the homes were now demanding greater access to a life outside the domestic sphere.

The Magic Bus team also worked to get the support of the local schools. These schools initially resisted the idea of the program because they thought it would take time and attention away from their education. But if the Magic Bus team could convince the school teachers and headmasters that inculcating activity-based learning was a valuable tool in building engagement and excitement for the school, teachers would begin to see the program as a teammate and not an opponent. If done correctly, this would lead to higher school enrollment and greater Magic Bus participation by children, which is another pillar of the Magic Bus program.

From experience, the Magic Bus team knew that once teachers and school administrators saw how much better the children were getting at learning and the sense of community that the Magic Bus program was creating, they would begin to warm up to the idea of working together. So, instead of practicing at the larger play spaces further from the schools, Magic Bus decided to run programs strategically close to or even within the schools, many times sacrificing comfort and space to be close to the schools. They wanted teachers to pass the children's groups on their way home. They wanted community members to see the game and want to be a part of it. This strategy continues to work to this day, slowly showing school administrators how a Magic Bus program can make their jobs easier and more fulfilling, and not harder and more stressful.

The last hurdle, now that they had enough buy-in to get girls into the program, was to make sure they stayed. And to do that, they had to convince the boys that it was in their interest to learn and play with the girls. Because this was the first time that the girls had ever been on a field, the boys were far more skilled. So how could they ensure that the girls could contribute in a meaningful way?

Magic Bus volunteers and staff began by making each team co-ed and mandating that all the teams must have a relatively equal number of girls. Two youth

66 Case Studies

mentors, one boy and one girl, would lead the formation of every team. Unfortunately, they learned that this wasn't enough. Once they got on the field, the boys would simply not pass to the girls. After a number of failed attempts to "create" teamwork, the Magic Bus team decided to go directly to the source. They created a youth council of boys and girls and posed the question to them: what could the program do to make sure girls are more engaged in the games? The youth council came up with a lot of great ideas that the program tried and tweaked. They finally landed on one idea that was used to level the playing field for girls

It was a modified version of a "magic goal."

Typically, if you play with magic goal rules, it means that you manipulate the value of a goal. The youth council decided that during a certain period of time, if a girl scored a goal, it would be worth two points. They quickly learned that the boys would only pass to the girls during that period of time. So they came up with a "secret" magic goal rule that meant that only the referee would know if it was magic goal time. Then, the boys would be incentivized to pass to the girls at all times in hopes that if they scored, it would be during the magic goal period.

In 2015, the Magic Bus program serves more than 300,000 children and youth from marginalized communities living in slums and villages across India. Over the course of 16 years of listening to and working with the communities themselves, today 46% of Magic Bus participants are girls. All because of how they changed the game.

Elements of Re-Design

- **Roles:** Encourage and enable mothers (and grandmothers) to play to demystify myths.
- **Rules of the League:** Males and females both need to be educated on gender equality, so every team must be co-ed. In addition, two youth mentors are charged with forming every team. Those mentors MUST be a boy and a girl.
- **Rules of the Game:** In an attempt to recalibrate the game and prevent boys from dominating, boys and girls on a youth council created their own version of a "magic goal." The referee knows there is a certain window of time during the game that a goal scored by a girl is worth 2 points. Nobody else knows when "magic goal" is happening.
- **Playing Area:** Schools don't typically support sport, at least at the outset. So, programs are purposefully set up in a visible area near the main center of the village or slum, near the school, to attract positive attention. Often, this is despite the fact that there are spaces better suited for sport further away.

USA Hockey and Cross-Ice Hockey

Until recently, if you took a trip to a hockey rink in the early hours of a Saturday morning, you would find two teams of players, as young as eight years old, playing in a regulation hockey rink. Compared to their small stature, the ice seems massive. On the ice, you'd see two kinds of kids—those who have more technical skill and athletic ability, and those in need of more of both. But the players in need of more time, practice and touches on the puck in order to develop skills would likely not get any of those things on this Saturday. The big rink suits the more skilled and athletic among the players so, on a game day, they are the ones who will be the most involved in the play. Because the game, even for 8-year-olds, closely mirrors the professional game, coaches would be focused on winning and not on the fundamental skills aimed at the long-term development of the players.

Fortunately, since about 2000, USA Hockey, the national governing organization for hockey in the United States, has been looking at these issues more closely. They realized that they weren't getting an optimal amount of skill development in young players because too many Saturday game days were being derailed by a hyper-focus on winning. And too many kids were dropping out because of it. They were losing some of the very children that they hoped would be the next generation of Olympic hopefuls and professional-caliber players.

FIGURE 5.2 USA Hockey

Credit: USA Hockey, Inc.

68 Case Studies

But changing an entire system is no easy task. Since 2009, Ken Martel, USA Hockey's Technical Director, and Kevin McGloughlin, Senior Director of Hockey Development, have been charged with changing the game of hockey to expand the player pool. This means that they concurrently needed more kids to start playing hockey, keep playing hockey and develop better hockey skills. Ultimately, the outcome they were most interested in was retention: do 8-year-olds come back to play as 9-year-olds?

As they dug into what was keeping them from achieving these outcomes, they realized that the reason that kids were leaving hockey or stalling in their hockey development had a lot to do with coaching and the structure of leagues at the youth level. Ken explained, "Your competition structure affects what you are going to do in practice." Because youth leagues were structured in a way that mirrored the professional model, it was no surprise that games and, even practices, were all pointing towards the same outcome: winning. The competition structure incentivizes the practice structure. And because coaches want to win, they teach in practice the things needed to be successful in competitions. In this case, that means giving many more opportunities to kids who show some athletic talent or early proficiency with the game.

Wanting to deliver an experience to participants that would keep them coming back, USA Hockey began to experiment with cross-ice hockey. Cross-ice hockey is essentially turning the game of hockey sideways in the rink, using the three zones as smaller rinks—small-sided games played by small people (usually the under-8 age group). The size of the rink is "right-sized" for the participants and because there are fewer players on each team, each player gets more opportunities to be involved in the play. "In an optimal cross-ice game plan, U8 (age 8 and under) children would spend five minutes warming up in each zone, then play a 17-minute game with a one-minute break in between sessions and then rotate through each third of the ice playing two other opponents. The games would work like any regular hockey game, but with quick face-offs used after goals, and coaches changing lines every 90 seconds or so."[1] Ken, Kevin and their team experimented with many variations of cross-ice hockey before coming up with a refined version that was both fun and helped kids develop skills.

As more leagues started to adopt the cross-ice format, USA Hockey started paying special attention to retention. Because most leagues run their registrations through USA Hockey, they were able to clearly see which 8-year-olds were returning as 9-year-olds. They started to see a pattern develop—those leagues that used cross-ice hockey had more returning 9-year-olds than those that didn't. In 2014, the leagues that used cross-ice hockey most of the time had retention rates of 88%–92%; those who used it only about half the time had retention rates of only 53%.

Despite the fact that USA Hockey has an extraordinary amount of influence in the youth hockey world—95% of youth hockey leagues are members of USA

Hockey—convincing leagues to change to the cross-ice hockey format was not without bumps in the road. Even with data that showed that cross-ice hockey was more enjoyable to the participants, that they had more ice time and therefore more chances to build hockey skills like decision-making, stopping, starting, changing direction, and shooting, still some parents remained skeptical. Parents were reticent because they feared that this different version of hockey would somehow shortchange their child's long-term development. And even though a desire to enhance players' long-term development was precisely the reason that USA Hockey introduced the format, parents still said, "But it's not real hockey." It took some time, but as parents started to see their kids play more and enjoy playing more, they became less resistant.

Parents weren't the only ones resisting the cross-ice hockey format. Surprisingly, rink owners, who feared that their economic model was in jeopardy, also lashed out against the change by not allowing their rinks to be used for cross-ice hockey. However, when USA Hockey developed portable sub-dividers, similar to gymnasium dividers on a basketball court, rink owners saw the potential of being able to rent out their spaces to multiple groups at a time and were completely won over.

At this point, cross-ice hockey is so popular that a recent tournament nearly filled a professional arena in Chicago. USA hockey is, as Ken Martel puts it, "past the tipping point." Now on any given Saturday morning, you'll find a hockey rink full of kids, most of whom are actively engaged in the game. They are learning skills, and they are having fun. Cross-ice hockey is no longer the exception, but the norm.

Elements of Re-Design

- **Playing Area:** Smaller space allows for multiple games across the ice at once. The boundaries were rubber bumpers originally, but now many rinks have cross-ice boards.
- **Equipment:** Puck changes and smaller goal size.
- **Rules of the League:**

    - No stoppages in play.
    - Games can be organized with goals facing in different directions to pose different challenges to scoring and defending.
    - Length of the game is 17 minutes, 1 minute of rest, start next game.
    - Each team plays three games.
    - To keep the game moving, referee or coach just introduces a "new puck" or frozen pucks after goals are scored.

70 Case Studies

Play Rugby USA

On a Monday morning in the late spring of 2008, a small group of middle-school rugby players wandered off the playground and into school when the bell rang. Having played in the first rugby tournament of their lives, they were all smiles. The school's assistant principal, who knew that the team hadn't had much success that year, had worried that the team would return disappointed having made an early exit from the city-wide tournament. After all, teams at the tournament had been playing together for multiple seasons, unlike P.S. 153's team which had just started a few months ago. Instead, when she asked the team how the tournament went, they practically screamed, "We made the playoffs!" And they had. But not because, as in the movies, they had all of a sudden received a divine intervention that made them into proper rugby players. Instead, they made the playoffs because of the very intentional work of the tournament organizers, the staff of Play Rugby USA.

When Mark Griffin started Play Rugby USA in 2003, there was very little, if any, youth rugby happening in New York City. It was well before the announcement in 2009 that Rugby Sevens would be an Olympic Sport. Interest in the game was not high. But Mark knew that rugby, if offered in an intentional way, could really take hold in public schools. He saw the huge potential for the game to grow and for those kids who aren't immediately drawn to basketball, baseball or football, to develop a love for this fast-paced, exciting game.

When you introduce a sport to kids who aren't familiar with the sport (and in many cases the kids in New York had never seen nor heard of rugby before), you quickly become conscious of the fact that in order to stick with something that is new, kids need to experience some progress. Being new at a sport and not being able to accomplish any of the goals of the sport doesn't make the game very fun. Neither does sitting on the sideline or waiting in line for your turn to get into the action. Mark and his team knew that in order to keep kids playing, they would need to overcome these challenges and make sure kids felt some success and had fun.

To do this, they set their rugby teams and leagues up so that any number of kids could play a match on any kind of surface. Much of the fun of sports is playing games, so Play Rugby USA made sure that, no matter what the attendance at a particular game, no team would need to forfeit. Matches could be 5 vs. 5 players, 7 vs. 7 or any number of kids available. Furthermore, games could be played outside on a field, inside in a gymnasium, or even on the dirt of a baseball diamond so that kids wouldn't miss the chance to play games simply because their school didn't have access to a pitch.

These changes helped keep kids interested and engaged in rugby. But on the eve of their first city-wide tournament, Mark and his team worried that all the good work they had done would be diminished by the results of this end-of-season event. Typically, tournaments or playoffs are held at the end of the season. Some predetermined number of teams enter the tournament and compete to be the last team standing. A team's ranking in the tournament determines who they will play, and often, those teams that have been successful throughout the season

FIGURE 5.3 Rugby USA

Credit: Mike Lee / TaiwanMikePhoto.com

72 Case Studies

earn the right to play against a lesser-skilled team. Even when tournaments include all the teams in a league, most tournaments are set up so that those teams that haven't had much success throughout the season will also likely have little success in the tournament. Mark and his team knew that this just wouldn't work. Some teams in the tournament had been playing together for a few seasons, while others were brand new. Some teams had lots of interested players, while coaches of other teams struggled to get enough kids interested in this new game.

Wanting all of their rugby players to finish the season on a high note, Mark and his team designed their tournament to encourage kids to come back and play more rugby. They would get more opportunities to work on their skills, and they would have as many chances as possible to face off against teams at their same skill level. Here is how the tournament works: All teams would participate in a first-round set of games, organized like a round robin. Then, all the teams that won all of their first round games would be entered into a group that won all of their first round games. All the teams that lost all of their first round games would be entered into a group with other teams that lost all of their first round games. Teams would be matched up against other teams that had a similar level of success in the first round. Then, the teams who all won their first round games would now compete against each other for the "Plate"- the trophy for that group. Those who lost all of their first round games would now compete for the "Cup." Those who won most of their first round games would compete for the "Golden Ball," etc.

Play Rugby USA's simple but intentional tournament design ensured that every group of teams, even those who hadn't won a game all season, had something to play for—that every game would matter. And because teams would be matched against teams of similar skill, these second round games, or the "playoffs," would be the time when teams would likely have their most evenly matched games. Most importantly, every team would go home feeling like they had been successful. And the next year, when sign-ups for Rugby would start again, every kid would remember that the previous year, they had "made the playoffs."

Elements of Re-Design

- **Playing Area:**
    - Games can be played on any surface of any size.
- **Rules of the League:**
    - Teams can be made up of any number of players (5 vs. 5, 7 vs. 7, etc.) depending on how many players are available.
    - At the end of the season, the tournament will be structured so that each team makes it out of group play and competes in elimination rounds; against teams with the same group play records of wins and loses.

United States Tennis Association

The kids in the first video looked like all the 10-year-old aspiring tennis players that Kirk Anderson, the Director of Coach Education for the United States Tennis Association (USTA), had seen at parks across the country. They would swing and miss with their unwieldy racquets. When they did make contact, the direction of the hit ball was unpredictable. They would rarely, if ever, hit the ball over the net. The concept of volleying back and forth between two players looked to be a reality only for the distant future.

The 10-year-olds in the second video were another story. They had clearly had more practice and better coaching. They swung their racquets with purpose, and the balls they hit went where they wanted them to go, namely to the other side of the court. They had the strength to hit the balls over the net and were volleying back and forth like a real tennis match.

After the second video, the Director of Coach Education for the Royal Belgian Tennis Federation addressed the group. A taskforce of coach educators from the world's largest tennis federations, including the "grand slam" countries—France, England, Australia and the United States—were gathered in London to address the collective concern that not enough youth were playing tennis.

The director asked the group what they thought of the two videos. The coach educators wanted to know how the kids in the second video were being trained. Why were they so much better than the first group? Were they in an elite program? Had they been playing for longer? The director answered that the same kids were depicted in the two videos, and that they were filmed on the same day. The kids in the first video played on a regulation-sized court and with full-sized racquets. The kids in the second video played on a smaller court with modified racquets. The change in their performance was immediate. This, the director proposed, was the way to get kids to keep playing tennis.

Kirk Anderson was sold. Like his colleagues in the room, he had been thinking about how to engage more kids in tennis for years. He knew that part of the problem in the U.S. was that tennis was a sport that not every kid could access. It requires expensive equipment and access to courts, which aren't always widely or publicly available. But Kirk found that even when they could eliminate those barriers, there was still something about tennis that didn't capture kids' excitement. That something was the fact that tennis required an extreme amount of skill and strength for the youngest participants to be successful.

The idea that you could change the equipment and court size spoke directly to the challenge of kids feeling successful. When they played with equipment and on courts that were designed for adults, they weren't successful. If they could start to see themselves getting better and get more quickly to the fun part of playing with another player, maybe they would want to stay. So despite the fact that the game of tennis had only seen six rule changes since the comprehensive set of rules were established in 1924, Kirk Anderson came back from London determined to bring with him to the USTA right-sized equipment and space for the youngest players.

74 Case Studies

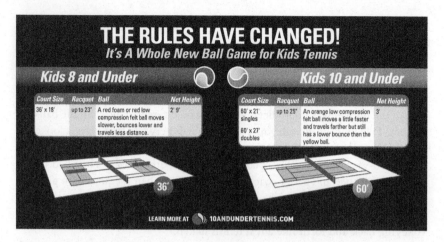

FIGURE 5.4 Illustration of changes made to USTA 10 and under tennis
Credit: United States Tennis Association

Now the challenge would be to get everyone in the U.S. on board. Anticipating some resistance at the community level, Kirk went first to his internal training team. These were Kirk's closest colleagues, and he knew that they also prioritized growing participation. After he explained, most of them took to the changes and incorporated them into their coach and community trainings. As Kirk said, "I was really lucky I had such a great group of national trainers. And they were so respected in the community that the changes started to spread pretty organically."

But not everyone supported the idea. Some community-level tennis professionals didn't want to incorporate anything that didn't look exactly like the tennis they were familiar with, for fear that it would stunt the development of the younger players. They were particularly resistant to another change that Kirk started to implement, a modified tournament structure.

In tennis, players are ranked for tournaments and follow a traditional format, where the highest seeded players face off against the lower seeded players. Kirk and his team thought that this practice stood in the way of kids getting more court time. And court time meant the chance to keep improving. They proposed that, instead of rankings, they would use round robin tournaments, and that they would modify the scoring so the games moved more quickly. This meant more time for more games for each participant. It also shortened games where there was a dramatic mismatch of skill (which often means someone is being "blown out").

Some tennis clubs chose not to change their format. But because Kirk and his team were well-respected and able to leverage the influential USTA brand, more and more places started to adopt the changes. When word spread that the changes really did mean more kids playing and more active engagement from younger participants, resistance started to fade. While there are still some places where you can find the more traditional structures, all official tournaments for the U8 and U10 (ages eight and under, ages 10 and under) divisions have these modified formats.

Now, courts all over the country from South Central Los Angeles to Miami Gardens in Florida are filled with kids who look like the stars in that second video.

Elements of Re-Design

- **Equipment:** All equipment is adjusted to three age and skill ranges: three different-sized racquets and balls correspond to the size, age and experience of the youth. Racquets are lighter and smaller. Balls are lighter, larger, and don't bounce as quickly or as high. Nets are not as high.

- **Playing Space:**
    - Court Size: Youth playing in the U8 (eight and under) age group play on a 36ft court; youth playing in the U10 novice divisions play on a 60ft court; youth playing in an open U10 league play on a regulation court.
    - "Pop-up" Courts: Transportable nets and lines that can be used on any surface.

- **Rules of the Game:** The games and matches are shorter for younger players.
- **Rules of the League:** The traditional tennis ranking system is not used for young children. All children play in a round robin tournament.

Street Soccer USA

"We've never had the illusion or pretense of developing athletes. Our work has always been about something more." Street Soccer USA's (SSUSA) mission is to "improve health, education and employment outcomes for the most disadvantaged Americans by using sports to transfer the skills necessary so they can achieve these outcomes for themselves." Serving primarily homeless adults and at-risk and homeless youth in 16 U.S. cities, SSUSA has pioneered the use of sport as a platform for meaningful personal transformation and social change.

The fact that they play for more than "the win" when they play soccer features prominently in the story of the creation of one of the most fascinating

FIGURE 5.5 Players celebrate as referees award green card
Credit: Street Soccer USA

re-Design stories we have uncovered. It is the story of SSUSA's Lawrence Cann and the remarkable "Green Card."

Each SSUSA team is based in a different city around the USA. They train independently and compete against local teams in their respective cities. Once a year, all of the teams travel to one city for the National Cup tournament. The first tournament was held in Charlotte, NC, in 2007. The SSUSA team worked tirelessly to make the event everything they aspired for it to be. They took care of logistics and tournament structure and uniforms. They worked to foster a special tournament atmosphere of openness and trust and safety. They set up the fields. They hung the banners. They pumped up the soccer balls. And when the time came for the first matches of the tournament, they suddenly realized they had not recruited any referees!

Lawrence jumped on the pitch along with someone from the crowd who happened to be a professional referee. The tournament was a huge success and upon reflection, the SSUSA team realized that the quality of the referee made a significant difference in the quality of the match, from the rule enforcement to the protection of players to the contribution towards a uniquely safe climate in the matches.

In 2012, the National Cup moved to New York. With the mission of the organization in the forefront of their minds, the SSUSA team began to revisit and scrutinize more elements of the tournament, searching for ways to amplify the player experience and to provide even more positive reinforcement to their players.

SSUSA was committed to preventing their players' soccer experience from recreating any of the intense marginalization that they too often experienced in their day-to-day lives. SSUSA is about rewarding good behavior; so many players talk about what it is like to play in an environment that so consistently offers positive reinforcement. Lawrence and his team realized that the idea of the red and yellow cards that referees issue as punishment in soccer matches were antithetical to their entire program model. The question was posed: What if these cards could reinforce good behavior? In Lawrence's words, "It took about one second after we posed this question to realize that the Green Card was the obvious answer."

On the first day of the 2012 tournament, the referees gathered to be briefed on the tournament rules. The original idea for using the Green Card was that at the end of the match, the referee would award one Green Card to the team that demonstrated the most pro-social behavior and SSUSA values. However, before the first day of the tournament was over, referees, on their own, had begun to give out Green Cards *during* matches as a way to recognize exceptional behavior in the moment.

Because it so nicely promotes SSUSA's mission, the leadership, staff, referees, coaches and players have made it an integral part of SSUSA's National Cup. Green Cards are a critical part of the tournament structure. In the case of tie matches, the team that has earned the most Green Cards is awarded the win. But it's more than that. SSUSA believes the Green Card also has helped to temper competitive tension that can escalate in matches. It's part of the organization's ethos. Together, stakeholders consider all the best ways to use it to achieve the best possible outcomes. It's such a part of who they are that they have even made it a part of the external leagues they run to raise money for SSUSA.

SSUSA has conducted a formal evaluation of the Green Cards in its tournaments, and their impact has been far reaching. Players and coaches tell many stories about how the desire to help your team earn a Green Card has motivated players to shift their behavior. For a population of players who are marginalized in society, who often are dealing with the effects of trauma and who are working on creating "small wins" in their lives, the Green Card presents a unique opportunity to be recognized and rewarded for doing something positive. Every coach mentioned the Green Card and how it gave them an easy and powerful way to talk about fair-play and to tangibly emphasize it.

The other crucial feedback has come from referees. Suddenly they felt like the "good guys," almost like social workers themselves. Many referees mentioned that the Green Card has empowered them and given them a special tool that they can use to directly contribute in healthy ways to the tournament. One referee was quoted as saying, "No one has ever cheered for me before when I have given red or yellow cards, but when I awarded Green Cards, seeing the players smile and hearing the crowd cheer for the Green Card actually made me feel good and simply made the refereeing more gratifying."

The Green Card has served as a poignant reminder to everyone of the SSUSA mission and values.

78 Case Studies

Elements of Re-Design

- **Equipment:** A Green Card, the same size as traditional yellow and red cards, is included in the referee's kit.
- **Roles:** At the referee's discretion, a Green Card can be given to recognize pro-social behavior and actions that embody SSUSA's values and curriculum.
- **Rules of the League:** Referees record Green Cards issued during a tournament match. In the case of a tie, the team with the most Green Cards is awarded the win.

World Rugby: Rugby Sevens

In 1883, in the town of Melrose, Scotland, a local butcher knew that his rugby club—the Abbey Club—was in dire need of money to enable it to survive. He thought hosting a rugby tournament might help him infuse some funds into the club. But this wouldn't be just any rugby tournament. He planned a shortened, modified tournament, thinking that more people would come to watch a one-day tournament that involved many teams instead of the usual few. He also thought that a shortened, modified game would help get more people excited about the tournament. He was right: the event was a huge success and this modified version of the game, Rugby Sevens, became increasingly popular.

Rugby Sevens is different from traditional Rugby Football in some key ways. First, instead of 15 players on the field for each team, there are only seven players per side, but the field is the same size. The action is less constricted than it is in traditional rugby, where much of the time and strategy is devoted to a laborious, hard-fought struggle for possession of the ball. In traditional rugby, high scores and long spectacular runs are difficult to enact when there are two evenly matched teams. Sevens contains longer runs and more spectacular "tries."

Second, whereas traditional rugby matches last at least 80 minutes, Sevens matches are only 15 minutes, seven minutes per half. Because the games are shorter, that means that matches usually stay closer in terms of the score, thus increasing interest and drama for fans and players. Further, it means that more games can be played during a set timeline, like a tournament.

Steve Griffiths, Head of Organizational Development at World Rugby, notes that among the major differences between traditional rugby and Sevens, "decision making is different; it is faster, and different types of decisions are being made." When there are fewer players, each has to pick up a larger share of the decision making. Furthermore, the game is played at a faster pace, so each player is more likely to be focused on decisions at every moment.

These changes, to the number of players and the length of a match, opened up the game. The smaller number of players led to more dynamic results on the field.

The shorter matches brought more interest in and engagement with the game—more people started to get involved. What started as a way for the Abbey Club to raise funds to sustain their club has become a massively popular version of the game. Sevens' popularity really took off in England at the end of the Second World War. It grew rapidly in popularity as an end-of-season "festival" day of exciting and quick rugby in which major and minor rugby clubs could participate. By the early 1970s, the Middlesex Sevens, in Middlesex, England, had become the largest Sevens tournament in the world, with nearly 300 teams competing.

Rugby Sevens also became a powerful medium for introducing the game of rugby to a worldwide audience. Some of the smaller rugby-playing nations of the 116-member World Rugby Organization realized that they could be more competitive at the Sevens game than at the traditional game despite their more shallow talent pools. It was also a game that appealed to less traditional rugby-playing countries, particularly in Asia. The rise in interest in Sevens during the late 1970s and 1980s in Singapore helped catalyze the sport to its current state of popularity. The establishment of the Hong Kong Sevens tournament, now one of the most prestigious tournaments in the Rugby World Sevens series, became a way for clubs to form teams to play in their off-season and to hone and showcase the skills of their players in need of further development.

No one person is responsible for the development of Sevens. Instead, it's evolved both organically at the local level and strategically from the influence of World Rugby, which recognizes the power to leverage the game's popularity to

FIGURE 5.6 Rugby USA

Credit: Mike Lee / TaiwanMikePhoto.com

80 Case Studies

grow the sport of rugby as a whole. In 2009, the International Olympic Committee voted to include Rugby Sevens on the program for the 2016 Olympic Games. And now that Rugby Sevens is an Olympic sport, its popularity might one day even overtake that of the traditional, 15-a-side format. Who would have thought that a game first played in a small town in rural Scotland would make its way to the world stage of the Olympics?

Elements of Re-Design

- **Rules of the League:**
  - 7-a-side: Only three can be forwards who participate in the scrum.
  - Length of the Match: Shorter halves, halftime and games.

Summary

While these six case studies span a wide variety of contexts, some common themes emerge. They highlight some of the things that you, as a Sport System Re-Design practitioner, should be aware of as you embark on your own designs.

Allies and Adversaries

Whether or not a re-Design succeeds has much to do with who is involved in its conception and implementation. Perhaps more than any of the other examples, the Magic Bus team was faced with the challenge of involving the right people at the right time. Unexpectedly, it was the mothers and grandmothers who were the high leverage point for getting more girls involved. And once they were involved, the team made the critical decision to include the kids themselves when trying to solve for the problem of boys not wanting to play with the girls.

Ken Martel and his team at USA Hockey ran into resistance from unexpected stakeholders. They anticipated having to convince parents that their new cross-ice format would deliver a positive experience that would help their kids improve their skills. But they didn't suspect that they would have to convince the rink owners to support the model. Had they not been able to introduce the bumpers and make the case that rink owners could also benefit, it would have been exceedingly difficult for USA Hockey, even with their huge influence on the youth hockey world, to implement their changes on a large scale.

Role and Control

The role of the person proposing the re-Designs influences their ability to make changes. In the cases of Kirk Anderson and Ken Martel, both were able to use

Case Studies **81**

their positions at the national governing bodies of their sport to motivate people to adopt their re-Designs. But as Kirk pointed out, many of the individual tennis clubs that operated independently of the USTA didn't have to implement their changes. They could run their programs and tournaments as they liked, so instead of *mandating* changes, they had to give them *incentives*. They had to convince stakeholders that the changes would bring about positive outcomes, and that fears that the new game wasn't "real tennis" or "real hockey" were unfounded. They relied on evidence that the changes would bring about the commonly desired outcome of better skill development.

Mark Griffin of Play Rugby USA and Lawrence Cann of SSUSA were in a different boat. Both were the ultimate decision makers in how their programs were run. They met little resistance because, in the contexts they were working in, there were few stakeholders advocating for the "traditional" way of playing their sports. For Lawrence, the population of homeless men was unique enough that people didn't see a reason not to make changes to the way the game was played. In Mark's case, there were so few rugby purists in New York City public schools that they had freedom to do what they liked. The buy-in they needed was internal only and was accomplished by letting their teams have a voice in the process.

The emergence of Rugby Sevens is an interesting case because the control over the adoption of Sevens was both driven at the grassroots and highest levels of rugby. The spread of "festival days" that served as hosts to Sevens tournaments was truly a grassroots, word-of-mouth effort. But, as Sevens became increasingly popular, instead of being threatened by the game, World Rugby, the international governing body of rugby, came up with a strategy for leveraging the popularity of Sevens to grow the game of rugby as a whole. Had World Rugby not taken this approach, the spread of Sevens might still have continued, but it's hard to imagine that it would have become an Olympic sport.

High Impact Outcomes

Perhaps the most important lesson learned from our case studies is the power of certain outcomes to positively impact our sports in multiple, and sometimes unexpected, ways. USA Hockey, the USTA and Play Rugby USA were interested in a simple outcome that is core to every sport context: retention. And all three organizations knew that in order to keep more kids playing for longer, the kids had to experience some success. For Kirk at the USTA, that meant equipment and space changes that enable kids to volley with each other. Ken saw success as a more equal distribution of engagement with the game, which came down to kids getting more touches on the puck. For Mark, success was playing as many games as possible and making sure that youth were playing against people who had similar skills. All of these strategies would encourage kids to stay with the game longer.

Street Soccer USA and the Magic Bus offered populations that had been marginalized from their sports the opportunity to play. For them, the simple outcome

82 Case Studies

of participation would lead to much more profound outcomes. Participation in Street Soccer USA programming would give homeless men the chance to work with a team towards a common goal. It would give them a sense of belonging and pride in the contributions that they were making. For many, it would be the first time that they felt like they mattered. But in order to do that, they had to stay on the field, so good behavior had to be rewarded.

At Magic Bus, the staff wanted girls to participate so that they could see themselves as equal to the boys on their teams. The efficacy that they developed by playing could set them up to believe in themselves in other areas of their lives. This might help them see pathways for their futures that they never imagined. First, they had to get the girls on the field.

We hope that these stories have helped bring the concept of SSRD to life so that you'll be inspired to re-Design your sport. Further, we hope that they have prepared you to be conscious of the things that you must consider in order to be a successful re-Designer. In the next section, we'll introduce a methodology that will help you plan and execute your re-Designs. As you move through that section, we hope you will remember that an Olympic sport can be created by a butcher in rural Scotland, a solution for gender equality in India can come from getting moms and grandmothers on the soccer field, and that an entire generation of future tennis players can be inspired by simply making the equipment smaller. Profound changes can be made by one person with a great idea.

Note

1. Age-Appropriate Hockey. (n.d.). Retrieved April 27, 2015, from www.admkids.com/page/show/915458-age-appropriate-hockey.

Reference

Age-Appropriate Hockey. (n.d.). Retrieved April 27, 2015, from www.admkids.com/page/show/915458-age-appropriate-hockey.

6

THE SPORT SYSTEM RE-DESIGN TOOLKIT

Part One

The previous chapters in this book have been dedicated to introducing and explaining the "what" of Sport System Re-Design: defining what it is, mapping the five core domains of SSRD, presenting its origins and sources of inspirations, and providing in-depth and real case studies of SSRD in practice.

This chapter and the next are dedicated exclusively to the "how" of SSRD. Our aspiration in writing this book was not just to present you with a new framework and approach to achieving important outcomes in youth sport. Our ultimate goal is to equip you with as many tools and techniques as possible to conduct your own SSRD experiments in order to get the outcomes you are seeking in your program.

In these two chapters we will outline a 5-step SSRD methodology—what we term the "toolkit"—as well as share with you a set of important "re-Design considerations" that need to be managed to ensure that you can conduct the re-Designs that will make the most possible inside your program or organization.

Our SSRD toolkit is depicted on the next page.

There are several key lessons we have learned from the SSRD conferences we have run, the stories of frontline practitioners attempting to implement SSRD, and our own work in the field. These lessons frame our approach to this SSRD Toolkit.

- SSRD entails a change to an existing system, often a system that is deeply established and entrenched in the psyche and behaviors of many people. Change can be met with criticism or resistance, and you need to prepare for it. However, change also opens the door to exciting new possibilities for your program.
- Re-Design is inherently a collaborative process and is more efficient and more effective when worked on with other people.

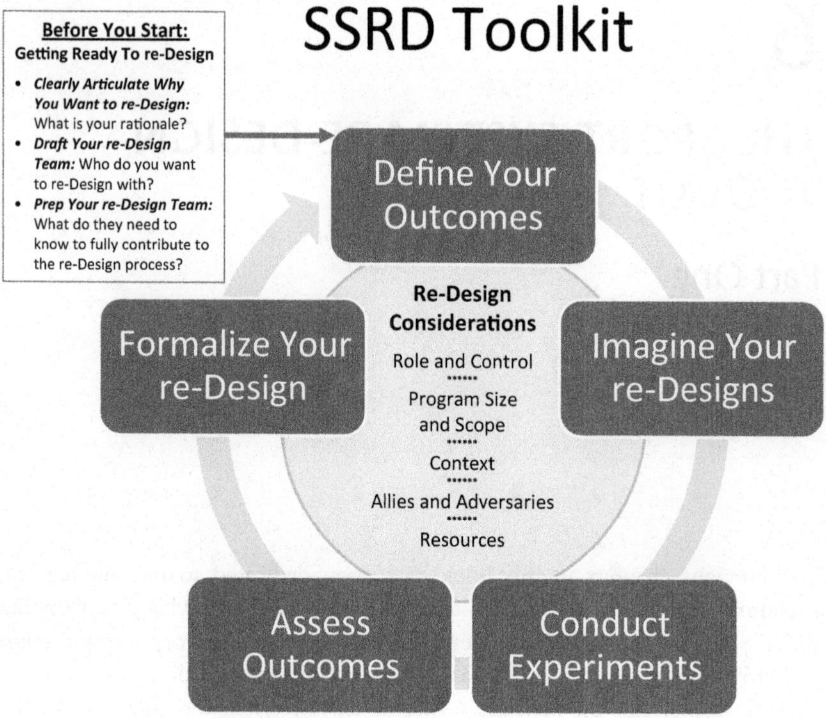

84 Sport System Re-Design Toolkit: Part 1

SSRD Toolkit

Before You Start:
Getting Ready To re-Design

- *Clearly Articulate Why You Want to re-Design:* What is your rationale?
- *Draft Your re-Design Team:* Who do you want to re-Design with?
- *Prep Your re-Design Team:* What do they need to know to fully contribute to the re-Design process?

Define Your Outcomes

Formalize Your re-Design

Re-Design Considerations

Role and Control
······
Program Size and Scope
······
Context
······
Allies and Adversaries
······
Resources

Imagine Your re-Designs

Assess Outcomes

Conduct Experiments

FIGURE 6.1 Sport System Re-Design Toolkit

- Players are often your most supportive and creative audience and can be the most receptive to re-Designs and changes in their sport. This makes them a valuable resource to the re-Design process.
- SSRD is an imperfect process and requires trial and error. It is creative, iterative and comes with unintended consequences and lessons learned. If you embrace it as a process rather than a quick fix, it can take you far.

The rest of this chapter introduces you to what to do before you start, and then works through the first two steps of our SSRD toolkit in detail.

Before You Start

We hope that at this point in the book your motivation for re-Design is high, and you are eager to make it happen in your league or program. Before you start, we recommend taking a few minutes to set yourself up for success in the re-Design process. This "pre-launch" step is crucial to a better re-Design experience and will help enhance your outcomes at the end of the process.

The three things we recommend you do in the "pre-launch phase" are:

1. Clearly articulate why you want to re-design
2. Draft your re-design team
3. Prepare your re-design team

Clearly Articulate Why You Want to Re-Design

When we first introduce individuals and groups to SSRD, there is often tremendous curiosity and enthusiasm about this approach. People can see the potential that SSRD holds for their program and the outcomes they aspire to achieve. They get excited by the examples we share and start to think almost immediately about how they can apply some of these examples to their program. We don't discourage quick experimentation, but we have found that taking the time up front to establish your rationale for SSRD makes the entire process more effective.

The first formal step in SSRD is to define your outcomes. Before doing that, it's important to be able to articulate what it is about this approach that particularly appeals to you. This helps you get buy in. The following questions will help you think this through. Document your answers, as you may find it useful to refer back to them. Consider:

- What is it about SSRD that energizes and/or interests you?
- What potential does SSRD hold for your program? Is there something that you think it might help you achieve that you haven't been able to accomplish?
- Does SSRD offer you something that traditional coach education or curriculum doesn't?
- Are there certain lightbulbs that have gone on for you as you've learned about SSRD?

Even as you recruit people to join you in your re-Design process, you may find yourself continually explaining what you are trying to do and what this particular approach is all about. It is important, therefore, that you can clearly articulate your interest in this process as well as what you think it can do for your program. Answering the questions above will help you form the foundations for what SSRD is and how it will work in your program, and the case you will make to people about why it is important.

Draft Your Re-Design Team

SSRD is a team sport. More brains, more eyes and more hands on the re-Design process is fundamentally better. It expands the idea pool and multiplies the perspectives from which the change can be viewed. What is more, it's just easier, more fun and more productive to try to re-Design your sport with collaborators.

86   Sport System Re-Design Toolkit: Part 1

Of course you can re-Design on your own, and you don't necessarily need a lot of people to come up with a great re-Design. What you need is the right people.

The right people are a diverse cross-section of:

- **Thinkers**: People with ideas, who can see the sport from many different angles and who believe that there are no sacred cows about the way a sport is played. They can invent and create and get excited about the idea of contributing to the "out of the box" thinking of re-Design.
- **Doers**: People who are the implementers of your re-Designs. These are often coaches, referees, players and fans. They understand the intention behind the re-Design and, when it comes down to it, are willing to give it their full effort to ensure the implementation is tried whole-heartedly.
- **Learners**: These are a special type of people who can step back and see the whole picture. They can observe the sport system and make accurate observations and evaluations about the impact of a re-Design. They can see unintended consequences and can make practical recommendations for tweaks to the experiments.
- **Champions**: People who believe in SSRD and are committed to making it work. These are the people who will defend and protect your re-Designs from detractors and will also advocate for and support your efforts. Champions could be Board members, respected coaches, activated parents and others.

Your re-Design supporters should grow as you begin to achieve successes. However, at the beginning, you want to build a small team who will work with you and support you leadership in your re-Design journey. At this phase, it is okay for the same person to fill more than one of the roles above.

Prep Your Re-Design Team

Your re-Design team will be more successful if they are adequately briefed and prepared for the re-Design process. To do this you need to do several things:

- **Articulate the "why" of re-Design for your program**: Why do you believe that SSRD is important and what do you hope it will accomplish?
- **Confirm commitment**: Make sure you explain to the re-Design team members what you are asking of them in terms of time, ideas and energy.
- **Orient the team to re-Design**: Provide them with the right background and context to understand SSRD before you start to brainstorm ideas. Explain where re-Design comes from and how it is different from other approaches. Choose your favorite examples of successful re-Designs to bring the concept to life. This book is a resource!

Sport System Re-Design Toolkit: Part 1   **87**

- **Invite cynics, more than once**: You actually want some cynics on your team. Their perspective is important, and they can offer views on re-Design that are important to hear. At first, they may not want to participate in a re-Design process. Ask them more than once and then be sure to be sensitive to what they need to know specifically to get excited about this process. Educate them about their role and the potential of what SSRD can do for your shared program.

After you have at least some of the members of your team in place, you are ready to start the formal process of Sport System Re-Design. You can carry out the formal steps individually, with discussions after each person on the team has worked through the steps, or you can address each step collaboratively from the start.

The Toolkit Step 1: Define Your Desired Outcomes

The first formal step in the SSRD Toolkit is to define the outcomes you are aspiring to achieve in your program. In its simplest form, an outcome can be defined as *something specific you want to achieve through your program or league*. There are all kinds of outcomes you may desire to achieve through your sport(s):

- Increasing the number of wins
- Improving a specific sport skill or life skill
- Reducing the number of fouls or violations committed by your players
- Increasing physical activity
- Reducing a type of injury or physical risk
- Making friends on a team

As we've noted in earlier chapters, and as you can explore in the Appendix, SSRD is practiced at all levels of sport, from professional to Olympic to collegiate to youth. As practitioners of sports-based youth development, our not-so-hidden agenda is to challenge readers of this book to find ways to achieve more youth-development-oriented outcomes through their sport work. These outcomes are not necessarily at odds with the desired outcomes of professional leagues.

For example, professional leagues often aspire to create the greatest parity between teams. Revenue and attendance suffer when games are blowouts. It is in a league's best interest to design for parity. However, parity is also essential in a SBYD program. Parity drives skill building, as teams that are well-matched will push each other to improve in an optimal way. Leagues with many close games can increase the motivation of players to continue to play, and this can enhance retention and participation.

88 Sport System Re-Design Toolkit: Part 1

At the youth development level, we have identified a core set of outcomes that SSRD can help achieve and that are commonly desired by SBYD programs. They include:

- Physical Activity
- Parity in Competition
- Participation and Retention
- Sport Skill Building
- Life Skill Building

We strongly recommend that your first experiments with SSRD focus on one of these outcomes. They are the easiest to achieve through SSRD.

Some socially conscious groups and sport-based programs are using sport to accomplish some remarkable aims. These are more complicated outcomes that are further removed from sport. For example, programs that work with homelessness, like Street Soccer, want to make an impact on a complex social problem. However, to build your capacity to both imagine and implement successful re-Designs, we encourage you to start with one or more straightforward outcomes from the list above. You will find that there are a great many important outcomes you can explore just from this short list. For example, how can we re-Design our sport:

- to provide at least 60 minutes of physical activity for every player?
- to increase girls' participation or increase retention of a certain demographic category of player who tends to drop out of our programs?
- so that there will be many fewer blowouts or lopsided games?
- to guarantee that every team/individual has a legitimate chance of making the playoffs?
- so that every player has the chance to improve their skills in every competition?

Clarifying your outcomes can be an intensive, in-depth process. For someone who is trying SSRD for the first time, it doesn't necessarily have to be this way. The following questions are a simple sequence that can help you get started clarifying the outcomes you want to achieve.

- **Outcomes Definition**: What do you hope to achieve through SSRD? How will you know that you have achieved the outcomes you desire? Remember to be as specific and detailed as possible.

  Example: A baseball and softball program in Los Angeles wants to ensure that every participant gets at least 60 minutes of moderate to rigorous physical activity during every baseball or softball game.

- **Outcomes Rationale**: Why do these particular outcomes matter?

  Example: In underserved neighborhoods in Los Angeles, too many kids are overweight or obese. They know the kids need 60 minutes of MVPA to stay healthy and fit. Further, they need to offer the opportunity to be active because the kids in their program are not getting this MVPA anywhere else in their lives.

- **SSRD Suitability Test**: Are these the outcomes that can be directly affected by the sport experience? If not, go back to #1 and re-articulate your desired outcomes.

  Example: Yes, because physical activity is already a part of baseball and softball, there *are* things that the program can change—maybe the playing area, rules of the game or roles—that might lead to increased physical activity.

- **Current Reality Check**: What are we already doing inside our sport that is helping us achieve these outcomes? Where are we not achieving the outcomes we desire?

  Example: Baseball and softball players don't achieve 60 minutes of MVPA during games because there are a lot of starts and stops and standing still waiting for the next play to begin. MVPA happens only when the ball is hit somewhere on the field.

Once you define your outcomes, you are ready for the next step in the SSRD Toolkit: imagining potential re-Designs

The Toolkit Step 2: Imagine Your Re-Designs

This is the ideation phase. This is when you are creating, inventing, exploring and brainstorming re-Designs and imagining how they could help you achieve the outcomes you outlined in Step 1.

This step in the SSRD process requires you and your re-Design Team to adopt a crucial set of *operating norms*. These norms should be introduced and explained before any brainstorming and re-Design meetings. They include:

- **Outcomes trump tradition**: In order to achieve this very important outcome, we are willing to re-imagine any part of our sport that may help us get there.
- **Nothing is sacred, unless we agree it is**: If there is a rule or part of the sport that we all deem as sacred and not up for re-Design, then we will name this and brainstorm on other parts of the sport. However, the best re-Design processes happen when no part of the sport is held sacred, and everything is up for re-Design consideration.
- **No idea is a bad idea**: The best ideas are rarely the first ideas, and the best ideas can often be born from ideas that came before them. This means that

90 Sport System Re-Design Toolkit: Part 1

it is vital to avoid discounting any idea shared by a re-Design team member. And especially with SSRD, because we are inventing new ways to play sports, protecting people and their ideas from critique at this stage is important.

- **Judgment and evaluation only comes after experimentation**: Because SSRD involves reinventing your sport, there is no way to know for sure if it will work until you try it. This is why the experimental step of this process is so crucial. It is too easy to discount an idea based on what you think may or may not happen when the idea is tried. But the only real evidence in SSRD is what you can see and hear inside your sport. This means that you must reserve judgment on any "ideas with potential" to after the time that you have seen the experiment in action.

Spark the Imagination of Your Re-Design Team

The re-Design stories that we recount in this book might seem inspired and ingenious. You can marvel at the creativity of the Green Card or the transformational power of cross-ice hockey. We also hope that in our case studies, we have conveyed the essence of the effort and time it takes to get a truly powerful re-Design. In other words, SSRD is less a matter of big ideas and more a matter of rigorous and persistent experimentation.

However, you do need some ways to fuel the creative thinking in your re-Design Team. It will not likely be as simple as gathering everyone in a room and saying, "Let's re-Design our sport. Go!"

SSRD is fundamentally about innovation and inspiration. To help fuel your creativity, and in the spirit of offering you a practical toolkit, we have gathered here some of our favorite techniques and approaches for fostering the imagination and thinking creatively about re-Design.

Seek Inspiration and Ideas From Actual Re-Designs

This book has partially been written to provide you with numerous examples from many different sports, within the U.S. and around the world and from the youth to the professional levels of sport play.

Re-explore different sections of this book. Look for inspiration in the case studies. Consider looking closely at the Appendix: at least one of the many examples is bound to resonate with you. There are many pages of inspiring re-Designs in:

- Sport re-Design: Historical Timelines of Popular Sports
- Examples of Invented and Adapted Sports
- Matrix of SSRDs

If something inspires you, try it out. Take one of the ideas from this book and ask yourself, "What would our version of this re-Design look like?"

Seek Ideas from the Sources of Inspiration for Re-Design

Chapter 4, "Sources of Inspiration," is full of groundbreaking ideas and examples of re-Design in places outside of youth sports. The ideas may not be sports-based, but if you look closely you may find that they help you and your re-Design team to think more creatively. The idea of moving the salad bar from behavior economics or the trim tab from systems thinking might inspire new ideas for the youth sport challenges you are trying to solve.

Play Games to Ignite Creativity

With your team, you can play a series of games to stimulate your thinking and ignite your new ideas. Here we suggest three approaches:

Same Game, Different Outcome: You introduce a common game that everyone knows. It's important that it's a simple game. For example, grab your re-Design team and play a game of beach ball "taps." Taps is a game where you and your team members hit the beach ball up in the air as many times as you can without letting it hit the ground. Challenge the group(s) to come up with ways to re-design the game for specific outcomes like more communication, higher levels of fitness and deeper competition. How would the team modify the game to get these outcomes? What would you change about the rules of the game, the roles of the players, the playing space or the equipment to get a different outcome?

Variations of this game could be played with 4-square or Tag. You might try versions of 4-square, like:

- 4-Square for skill development
- 4-Square for teamwork
- 4-Square for situational awareness

Or maybe your group likes Tag best. Try modifying Tag so that you get different kinds of outcomes, like:

- Tag for agility
- Tag for conflict resolution
- Tag for decision making

Once you have some re-Design ideas, then play out the game with each re-Design idea—in other words, practice experimenting with whether the re-Design works.

Flashback to Great Childhood Games: Think back on your favorite neighborhood games. Ask yourself:

1. How was the game played?

92 Sport System Re-Design Toolkit: Part 1

2. What was the objective?
3. What were the rules?
4. What playing area did you use?
5. What equipment did you use?
6. Were there specific roles people played?

Then, describe these games to your group. Talk about what specific positive things (outcomes) happened in the game. Try to uncover what specific designs contributed to these positive outcomes and push the team to remember what made those games fun and memorable. What was it about the game that made it compelling?

Use poster paper to write down the specific outcomes that resulted from playing the game. Then, write down what aspects of the five SSRD domains led to these outcomes. Brainstorm with the group what you could apply from these games to your re-design ideas.

Design a New Game: Another approach you can use to get your minds working might be to try to construct a new game. Provide the group with some sport equipment (balls, cones, etc.). The equipment could be familiar to the primary sport of your program or it could be from different sports. Challenge the group to create a *new* game using only the equipment provided. Give them a time limit to design and experiment with their game. Invite group(s) to teach everyone else their new game. You might consider providing groups with a specific outcome to focus on or some type of game requirement.

Spend Time Thinking About Other Sports

Keep in mind that getting in the re-Design mindset takes time. For most people, it's easier to think about other sports and the changes that can happen to sports that aren't your "own." This allows for more creativity in the process and results in more outlandish ideas. Those outlandish ideas are actually crucial to the process of imagining changes in your own sport. If you can do unconventional things to another sport, maybe some rule or equipment changes to your own sport won't seem so crazy.

Designing a Sport for a Specific Outcome: Assign groups to specific sports and a specific outcome to try to achieve through that sport. Challenge groups with outcomes that are not normally associated with that sport. Examples include:

1. Baseball/Softball for fitness
2. Soccer for (much) higher scores
3. Volleyball for individual touches
4. Skateboarding for teamwork
5. Rugby for conflict resolution
6. Tennis for (much) more parity in matches

Explain to your team that their task is to re-Design the sport to achieve these outcomes. Gather groups together to report on their re-Designs.

Borrow From Other Sports: Challenge the group to come up with ideas for one or more of the following "what if" questions:

- What if we took the shot clock in basketball and applied it to rugby?
- What if we moved the blue line rule from hockey into soccer?
- What if we took the net from volleyball and used it in tennis?
- What if we took the mercy rule from softball and used it in football?
- What if we took the structure of snowboard cross and applied it to cross-country?
- What if we took the non-stop play of rugby and tried it in football?
- What if you could have more than one person on a base in baseball/softball?
- What if we didn't tackle each other in rugby?
- What if a rowing race had forced substitutions halfway through the race?
- What if you earned points in the league standings for honorable behavior?

After the group has brainstormed answers to several of the above questions, lead a discussion about which ideas they liked the best and what it was like to try to re-imagine these aspects of sport differently. Challenge them to take some part of the sport your program plays and try to create a radical re-Design.

Brainstorm About Outcomes

All of the above exercises are intended to help you ignite the creative spark in your re-Design team. Many teams need to "play" with re-Design to get comfortable with this kind of reimagining of sport. After participating in one or more of these exercises, participants are often more comfortable, confident and clear about what re-Design is and how they can use it reimagine their sport.

At this point you are ready to tackle the specific outcome(s) you want to achieve through SSRD. Gather your re-Design Team together, present the desired outcomes and then facilitate them through an idea-generation session. Your goal is to gather as many ideas as possible—if possible, from all five domains of SSRD. You never know which domain may produce the most and best ideas that you can use to engineer your eventual re-Design. Depending on your specific outcome, some of the questions related to each of the five SSRD domains can prove useful:

Domain One: Re-Designing the Playing Space

1. Changing the size/shape of playing space

    a. What's the most age-appropriate space for our participants to play in? For safety? For ability?

94 Sport System Re-Design Toolkit: Part 1

    b.   Could changing the playing space facilitate increased action/participation/skill-building for each player?

    c.   What could happen if we made the space bigger? Smaller? Shallower? Steeper? Flatter?

2.   Changing the lines, boundaries or zones within the area of play

    a.   Can you change things about the playing area to adjust for skill or ability (such as the position of the three point line in basketball)?

    b.   Would changing something about the playing space allow you to promote or limit a certain behavior?

3.   Introducing or eliminating some permanent object or fixture in your playing area

    a.   What happens when an outdoor sport moves indoors?

    b.   Are there ways to decrease stoppages in play by changing the playing area (introducing walls in indoor soccer or the bumper in cross-ice hockey)?

    c.   Does anything about the playing surface need to be changed in order to promote safety or change the pace of play?

Domain Two: Re-Designing the Equipment

1.   Changing the size of the goals

    a.   Are there more or less points scored if you change the size?

    b.   Do other things about the game change if we change the goals?

2.   Adapting or re-Designing the existing or traditional equipment of your sport

    a.   Can you change equipment so that it is inclusive of all ability levels?

    b.   Are there safety issues that could be addressed through equipment changes?

    c.   What if you made the equipment bigger? Smaller? Out of different material?

3.   Introducing equipment from another sport

    a.   Are there aspects of other sports that you would like to highlight in your sport?

    b.   What if you played your sport with a certain kind of equipment from another sport?

4.   Creating new equipment for your sport

    a.   Is there something we could invent that would make our sport better?

Domain Three: Re-Designing the Rules of the Game

1. Re-imagined scoring

   a. How else could points be scored?
   b. How much could points be worth?
   c. Are there different point values for different aspects of the game?
   d. Are there ways of scoring we don't have now that we could add in?

2. Types of penalties/awards

   a. What types of violations or fouls should we have?
   b. What types of awards should we incorporate?

3. Consequences of awards/penalties

   a. What are players allowed to do when the other team commits a penalty?
   b. Are there behaviors we want to promote by implementing awards?

4. Limitations and restrictions

   a. What actions are possible (legal) during play?
   b. What actions are required during play? Why?

5. Starts/Stops/Restarts

   a. How can we increase or decrease the number of stops in a game?
   b. Would changing the restarts of a game change anything else about the game?

6. Number of players and substitutions on the team

   a. What if we changed the number of players in the competition?
   b. What if we changed our substitution rules? Or made substitutions automatically after a score or at a certain time during the game?

Domain Four: Re-Designing the Rules of the League

1. League/Competition schedule

   a. What does a "season" of your sport look like? How long should it be? How often should there be competitions relative to practices?
   b. Which teams play each other and why?
   c. What criteria determine standings?

2. Tournament/Playoffs format

   a. How do teams advance to the next round?
   b. What criteria determine league standings?

3. Duration of competitions

   a. How long do competitions last?

96 Sport System Re-Design Toolkit: Part 1

    b. Are there periods/halves/quarters? How long are they? How long is the intermission?

4. Built-in formats and behaviors

    a. Who shakes hands and when do they do it?

    b. Are there things that both teams do together? Like cheers or songs or dances?

    c. Are there rules in place that mandate a strictly followed behavior code for players or coaches?

Domain Five: Re-Designing the Key Roles in Our Sport

1. Referee/Umpire

    a. How can we make better use of the often highly skilled adult who participates in the game?

    b. How can we ensure that the referee/umpire is supporting our outcomes?

    c. What does the referee/umpire need to do to model good sports behavior?

2. Coach

    a. How can we make sure that the coach provides positive feedback before, during and after the game?

    b. How do we entice the coach to broaden their vision of success to more than winning?

    c. How can we get coaches to model good behavior? Advance play for both teams? Intervene with culture and traditions?

3. Fans

    a. What could we do with how we involve our fans that could promote a more positive contribution from them?

    b. How can we decrease the fans' focus upon winning?

4. Players

    a. Where could we design leadership/coaching/mentoring roles for our players?

    b. Where can we create opportunities for our players to contribute/matter?

    c. How do we increase player ownership over their behavior, the integrity of the game and the dynamics of their team?

While you are imagining your potential re-Designs, don't forget to document *all* of the ideas you come up with. A great re-Design is often born from many preceding ideas. And though the final re-Design may be just what you need, the ideas it took to get there may help fuel future re-Designs or tweaks you need to make to your current experiments in SSRD.

Finally, once you have a re-Design that you like, go back to your original desired outcomes and check to see how the re-Design would help you get there. Craft your Outcomes re-Design statement, which follows a simple formula, including statements such as these:

- This re-Design will help us achieve X outcome by . . .
- This re-Design will make it easier to . . .
- This re-Design can help us get more . . .
- This re-Design may help us to eliminate . . .
- I'm excited about this re-Design because . . .

Now you have worked your way through the first two steps of the Toolkit. You've defined your outcomes and imagined your re-Design(s). It's time to go to work with your ideas and seeing how they fare in your sport system.

7

THE SPORT SYSTEM RE-DESIGN TOOLKIT

Part Two

In Chapter 6 you got ready, planned, brainstormed and decided on your re-Design. In this chapter you will go through three steps that will take you into the actual process of making your re-Design real. You'll learn how to conduct experiments to see whether and how your re-Design actually works. You'll assess outcomes in order to refine your re-Design and to convince others of the value the change. And finally, you will learn about how to formalize your re-Design—how to make it a permanent part of your sport system.

The Toolkit Step 3: Conduct Experiments

Once you have your re-Design(s), it's time to start to experiment. A re-Design can look one way on paper and appear differently once it's put into your sport system.

Here is what we recommend for conducting re-Design experiments:

- **Experiment sooner**: It is important to imagine re-Designs, and it is equally important to avoid over-thinking your re-Designs. There is no better way to learn than to see your re-Design inside your sport system. If you have an idea that you like, try it sooner rather than later.
- **Experiment iteratively**: One try at your re-Design will not be enough. You may need to try it 10 or even 100 times with different variables until you start to see the results you want. Do not be afraid to conduct many experiments on the same re-Design. Each time you conduct the experiment you will learn something.
- **Keep the experiment small-scale at the start**: You may have big aspirations for what your re-Design can do; however, the odds are that it will

100 Sport System Re-Design Toolkit: Part 2

take a while to get there. When you start, start small-scale. The smaller the experiment, the more control you have over it, which means you can work with it while it is happening. That way you actually can create a faster way to learn from the experiment.

- **Start the experiment in a safe part of your sport system**: High visibility re-Designs invite critique. Find a part of your system that is out of the spotlight and run your first experiments there. This may be a league with younger participants or even a practice or scrimmage at first. Do anything you can to prevent cynics and system-internal resistance from infecting your experiment.

Once you have planned for your experiment, you are now ready to actually conduct it. During every round of experiments, keep the following guidelines in mind:

- **Be hands-on**: SSRD is an active and creative process. Though you want to control for certain variables, inevitably, once you put your re-Design into your sport system, there will be tweaks and adjustments you will need to make. Stay close to the experiment so you can learn and adjust as rapidly as you can.
- **Tinker throughout**: A corollary to being hands-on is to be willing to adapt during an actual re-Design experiment. Try to minimize the disruption to the actual competition, but otherwise, if you think you can adjust some element of the re-Design to immediately enhance an outcome, go for it!
- **Trust your gut**: Though you will be looking for real evidence of impact, you also need to trust your gut as you make decisions about the experiments you are conducting. If something doesn't feel right, or you have an intuition about some element of your re-Design, give it a try. SSRD is part scientific experiment, part creative endeavor.

Remember, re-Design experiments may need time. It might work out that your re-Design idea has immediate traction and impact. It might be that you need weeks, months or years to conduct the right experiments to get your new sport system to the place where it is achieving the outcomes you desire. Be patient. Be observant. And keep on experimenting.

The Toolkit Step 4: Assess Outcomes

You are choosing re-Design because you have some outcome you want to achieve in your sport system. You may want to make the experience more fun for participants, seek to improve the skills of your players or to increase retention. In order to truly utilize SSRD to its fullest, you must work towards assessing whether your re-Designs are helping you achieve the outcomes you desire.

The good news is that you are already quite skilled at assessment. As coaches or league administrators, we are constantly watching the players and the game and thinking about the adjustments and decisions that will help our players improve and have a better experience. What SSRD leaders do is turn on their existing observation and evaluation skills and use these skills to gauge the impact of these re-Designs.

Assessing for outcomes means paying attention to the experiment and asking yourself several simple but important questions:

- What are we getting from this re-Design experiment?
- What *aren't* we getting?
- Are we getting anything that we did not plan for?

In order to successfully assess your re-Design experiment, you need to:

- **Pay close attention**: Get close to the experiments you are making. Make notes about what you are seeing.
- **Make time to think about it**: Step away from the experiment and review your notes. Look again at your outcomes. What is working? What isn't working?
- **Talk about it and listen**: Talk with your re-Design Team. Talk to your players, coaches, referees, fans, etc., and collect their perspectives. This active way of engaging with the key stakeholders helps fill in the gaps of what you might not be able to observe. In particular, it will tell you about how the game changes have an impact on them.

Assessment is the key ingredient to refining and advancing your re-Design. You know you have conducted your experiment and assessment successfully when you have a re-Design that becomes embedded in your program. At that point you can move towards the final step in the SSRD Toolkit: formalizing your re-Design.

The Toolkit Step 5: Formalize Your Re-Design

Congratulations! If you've reached this stage of the process, your tinkering and testing paid off. You have a re-Design that will help your program achieve its desired outcomes. Now, it's time to make this new design an official part of what you do. This fifth and final stage of the Sport System Re-Design process is called Formalize Your re-Design.

There is no standard procedure for formalizing your re-Design. The extent to which you need to formalize your re-Design into the program depends, in large part, on the size, scope and set-up of your program. If you're the sole person in charge of all the domains of the sport system, then you might never have

102 Sport System Re-Design Toolkit: Part 2

to officially formalize your re-Design. More likely, though, there will be many people who are either directly or indirectly affected by your re-Design such as coaches, program staff members, parents, players and referees that will need to understand the re-Design well enough for it to become formalized.

You'll know your re-Design is formalized when it becomes an accepted part of the way you do things in your program/league. When you no longer need to remind the coaches, parents, or players and, in fact, they do it without you reminding them, that's when a re-Design is truly formalized.

Document it

1. Write specifically about your re-Design. Describe what it is, how it works and what outcomes you are achieving.
2. Write down your re-Design everywhere that you share information about your program or league.
3. Put it in your materials—in your curriculum, manuals, newsletters, etc.

Train to it

1. Start teaching people in your program/league about your re-Design.
2. Make it part of your coach training program; make sure your staff/volunteers understand your re-Design.

Share it Publicly

1. Tell people about it. Talk to your colleagues, coaches, parents and players and find out what they think.
2. Ask people to come and see your re-Design to gather additional feedback.
3. Take what you have written about your re-Design and send it to colleagues. Publish it on your website.

A Special Way to Formalize Your Re-Design: Evaluation

Evaluating your re-Design is not as difficult as it seems. Remember when you were "assessing" your re-Design by watching it, talking to people about it, and asking questions about it? That was a form of evaluation—"on-the-spot" evaluation. The only real difference between that more informal evaluation and this is that now you have to be more systematic and methodical about it. You'll try to remove opinions and get to facts.

The core elements of an evaluation include:

- Doing more than just on-the-spot assessments; create a way to formally measure outcomes.

Sport System Re-Design Toolkit: Part 2 **103**

- Measuring your outcome over time, not just at one point in time. You want to understand short-term and long-term impacts of your re-Designs.
- Potentially enlisting someone with evaluation expertise to help you figure how to conduct a formal evaluation of your re-Design.

There are two basic levels of evaluation to consider:

Level 1 Evaluation

When it comes to evaluation, we know you've heard a lot of jargon. Here, we're going to take out as much of it as we can—no talk of logic models, indicators, theories of change, validity or reliability. Instead we'll talk about three things you can do to more formally evaluate your program. We call this Level 1:

Observe it: When you were in the "assess" phase, you did on-the-spot observations to get a sense of whether or not your re-Design was working. Now, you can add a little more structure to those observations. You might:

1. Record your observations. Write them down or videotape them.
2. Choose specific behaviors you want to observe and track them.
3. Assign more than one person do the observations.

Count it: There's no clearer way to show a change in something than by counting it. There are lots of different ways to count things and even some tools that will help you get an accurate count. Some examples include:

1. During your observations, you might choose to count how many times a player or coach engages in a certain behavior.
2. In your sport, there might be a certain fitness or skill test that your players can complete.
3. Are there any aspects of your sport system that can be tracked by timing them? Use a stop watch to count how long a behavior lasts or is absent from your sport.

Ask about it: A crucial part of evaluating the success of the re-Design will be asking participants, observers or other stakeholders what they think of the re-Design and whether or not they observed the changes you intended to make. Create a standard set of questions to ask in focus groups, surveys or interviews. These questions could include:

1. What impact is this re-Design having?
2. What is different now compared to before we started using the re-Design?
3. What additional re-Design ideas could help us further achieve our desired outcomes?

104 Sport System Re-Design Toolkit: Part 2

A good example of using this sort of Level 1 evaluation was an exploratory study that Burton et al. (2011) conducted in a 3rd/4th grade flag football league in which 47 players competed. They changed two elements of the competitive structure in order to achieve the outcome of higher scoring games: 1) the size of the football was changed to a youth size and 2) they instituted a delayed count before the defender could rush the quarterback. The results revealed that scoring increased over 100% and attrition decreased by more than 50% compared to the previous season. The participants also completed a short survey following the season that attempted to gauge what they thought about the rule changes and whether they liked them. While this was an exploratory study, the researchers saw it as having the potential to pave the way for more experiments and evaluations of programs that matter to their participants.

Level 2 Evaluation

Once you've collected some of this data, the next step is to compare the data to something. There are three possible comparisons you can make:

Comparisons over time: Using the same process you used to collect your first set of data, collect a second set of data with the same participants at a future date. Compare the findings of the data to see if any changes have occurred.

Comparisons to another group: Using the same process you used to collect your first set of data, collect a second set of data with another group of participants. Make sure that the group is as similar to your participants as possible except for the fact that they haven't implemented your re-Design.

Comparison to a standard: In some cases, the instrument you used to collect your data might have a standard against which you can measure your program's success. For example, the Centers for Disease Control recommend that all youth receive 60 minutes of moderate to vigorous physical activity (MVPA) at least five times a week. If your players exceeded this standard, you could say that your program meets this health and wellness standard more than successfully.

Hopefully, as you read this book, you are finding that evaluation isn't as hard as you thought. All it takes is a little curiosity and some careful thought about how you can replicate the same things over and over again in different situations. Just to be sure it all makes sense, let's walk through, step by step, how we might evaluate a hypothetical re-Design:

Evaluation Example

Challenge: How can we change soccer so that there is more attacking play/ offense?

Re-Design: Institute the back-court rule from basketball into soccer. This means that players cannot play the ball back into their own end once they have crossed the half-field line. If they do so, they turn the ball over and the other team receives a throw-in.

Level 1 Evaluation

Observe it: Create a checklist full of things that show that a team is playing offense, e.g. number of goals scored, number of shots on goal, or number of corner kicks. Put a check mark next to each item when you see it happen in the game. Have two other people, maybe volunteers who don't know that you're trying to increase offense, fill out the same checklist to ensure that your check marks are accurate.

Count it: Use a stop watch to measure the amount of time during the game that the teams play offense. You can start the stopwatch while they are attacking and stop it for any stoppages in play or when neither team possesses the ball. See how much of the game is now accounted for by "offense."

Ask about it: Create a survey that asks questions about the incidence of playing offense, like:

1. Approximately how many shots on goal did your team take?
2. For what percentage of the game do you think your team played offense?
3. How often was your team penalized for passing the ball behind the half-field line?

Level 2 Evaluation

Comparison over time: Complete your observations, time measurement or survey at the beginning and end of the season. Look for changes in the amount of offense teams played.

Comparison to another group: Find another soccer league where participants of similar background participate in the traditional version of soccer. Use your observation tool, stop watch, or survey and see if there is a difference in the amount of offense with your re-Design or the amount of offense without your Re-Design.

Re-Design Considerations

Before we end this chapter, we want to present you with five considerations to keep in mind throughout your re-Design work. These are important because they can show up at any step in the process and often are present at multiple times, or consistently throughout. If we thoughtfully monitor and intentionally account for

106 Sport System Re-Design Toolkit: Part 2

them, they can amplify our impact. When we ignore or gloss over them, they can at best inhibit and at worst completely derail our re-Design work.

Five Critical Re-Design Considerations

Role and Control

Your position within the organization, program or league has an effect on the way you go about your re-Design. Typically, the greater formal authority you have, the more power you will have to advocate and even mandate re-Designs. If you have less formal authority, it may be more difficult. While role and authority aren't always linked, it's important to consider where in the organization you sit and how to get people in other roles on board with your re-Designs. Sometimes you can get things done, not because you are the boss, but rather because you are knowledgeable and committed to what works for the kids. The higher-ups know this because they see that the kids listen to you. So do not discount that you can get things done.

Separate from role, it is important to assess the degree to which you have control over your league/program. You may not have a high-standing role but may still have tremendous control in influencing the necessary stakeholders to adopt your re-Designs.

Program Size and Scope

The bigger the program, the more difficult it may be to implement a re-Design but also the greater the potential for the right re-Design to impact more participants. It is also important to think about the program's scope—the number of different parts of your program. If you operate in a context where there are many different programs operating at the same time, full-scale adoption of re-Designs may not be appropriate. Instead, you might need re-Designs that work for a specific set of participants or in a particular context. Will your re-Designs apply to every program within your organization? Or are there some re-Designs that will be implemented differently depending on distinctions like:

- recreational vs. competitive programs
- programs for younger vs. older age cohorts
- programs for girls vs. boys
- programs for players with low skill vs. those with very high skill
- programs for beginners vs. intermediates vs. experts

Context

It's important to understand the context in which the program you are looking to re-Design is operating. External factors within this context can influence your ability to make changes. For example, if you are operating a program in a context that is deeply rooted in the traditional ways of playing a certain sport you will encounter a different set of challenges than a person proposing to modify a sport with less tradition, profile and history in another community.

You will need to consider the programs and stakeholders around your program. Is there another sport league that acts as a "feeder" to your league? Is your program a "feeder" for another league? Will the people in these other places need to at least understand the modifications that you are making to your program? You will also want to consider what the landscape is like for people who decide that they don't want to be part of your league. Where will they go? Will it be easy for people to leave your league in favor of another? And if so, will that influence how unorthodox you choose to be with your re-Designs?

Allies and Adversaries

There will likely be at least a few core folks who believe in what you are trying to do and are genuinely interested in trying this new approach. As we mentioned above, you should do your best to cultivate a diverse and influential group of these allies. However, it's possible that there will be some people who don't support your re-Design. At the beginning of your design process, we actually encourage you to enlist people who you think might be skeptical to the process. They can provide valuable insight that should be weighed when you consider re-Designs. But later, once you've settled on a re-Design, you'll likely face some people who need to be convinced of the merits in order to move forward. This is where having evidence of the success of your re-Design might make a difference. You can also turn doubters into supporters by finding creative ways to educate all stakeholders on SSRD and by leveraging your existing allies to advocate for the approach. The more that people understand and experience SSRD, the more likely they are to be allies.

Resources

It will be important to consider what other resources, in addition to buy-in, brain power, and creativity, you will need in order to implement a re-Design. As you are recruiting people to the team, you'll want to consider and make clear what their commitment to the process is going to be. Maybe they will be part of the design team, or maybe they will be an "early adopter" coach who tries out the re-Design as soon as you are ready to pilot it. But you also might need to convince people who have control over how financial resources are allocated, the facilities, equipment or back office logistics. The success of your re-Design will rest, in large part, on your ability to bring the right kind of resources to the table.

The Final Step: Action

It's time to re-Design. You know what Sport System Re-Design is. You have hopefully been inspired by the case studies and examples. Now, you have the toolkit. You are equipped to make your mark on your program and hopefully on the emerging field of Sport System Re-Design. Our concluding chapter outlines our hope for this body of work and offers some future directions for where we could all go next.

However, we would not be offended if you were so excited to start re-Designing that you skipped our next chapter, the Conclusion, and got right to it.

Reference

Burton, D., O'Connell, K., Gillham, A. D., & Hammermeister, J. (2011). More cheers and fewer tears: Examining the impact of competitive engineering on scoring and attrition in youth flag football. *International Journal of Sports Science and Coaching. 6*(2), 219–228.

8

CONCLUSION

In this book we aspired to provide you with everything you will need to implement Sport System Re-Design in your league or program. We have shared with you the SSRD framework for how to go about re-Designing your competitive youth sport experience to get the specific outcomes you seek. We provided a rationale for why you should consider using this approach in looking to have a positive impact on your program or league. We offered many examples to inspire your own efforts as you embark on the journey. We described the SSRD toolkit, a detailed process to guide your efforts, from the first step all the way to formal re-Designs that become part of the culture and practice of your sport organization.

It's important to note that if you choose to embark on the pathway of re-Design, you will not be alone. There are like-minded people involved in their own re-Design experiments, and they are coming together through conferences, web-based meetings and we hope, around the dialogue that will form around this book. We are in the nascent stages of becoming a vibrant *community of practice*—a group of people who learn from one another by engaging together in an activity that serves their common interests and goals. Before closing this book we want to share where we are as a community of practice, the mindset shift we hope you'll leave with, and where we imagine the field of SSRD can go.

Community of Practice

We've been building our community of practice and gathering examples of re-Designs for five years. We first promoted the idea in John's *Sport Theory and Social Systems* class at the Boston University School of Education. We then held our first conference, the *Change the Game: Sport System Re-Design Conference* at Boston University in 2012. Through both venues, we have engaged

110 Conclusion

undergraduate and graduate students in generating re-Design ideas for practitioners from a wide range of organizations and entities, from Major League Baseball's RBI program to local SBYD programs.

We have facilitated the re-Design process at our conferences with groups of 60 to 125 participants, in Boston, New York and Los Angeles. We have done meetings and trainings with groups that are part of the Up2Us Sports national sport-based youth development network. And we have elements of the SSRD toolkit in our ongoing consultation with programs and leagues.

From each of these settings, there are practitioners who have been inspired and motivated to re-Design on their own. Below are some of our favorite examples:

Peabody, MA, Youth Basketball

Justin Barasso is a middle school teacher and basketball coach. As a student in John's class, he was introduced to the SSRD framework and later attended our conference in 2012. During the summer he directs a youth basketball league in Peabody, MA. In many ways Justin is in the ideal setting to implement SSRD because he has a high degree of control over how the league is set up, and it is small enough that he can experiment and be able to personally observe the ways that those changes play out.

Justin incorporated some elements of the Doc Wayne designs into the Peabody league, like the "teaching referee." He also incorporated how the ref joins the team huddle during timeouts and the practice of teams shaking hands *before* the game.

Boys and Girls Clubs of Boston—Unity Basketball League

Bethany Riley, Athletic Director of the South End Boys and Girls Club in Boston came to the first conference and later decided she wanted to bring SSRD to her clubs. Bethany organized a meeting of the athletic directors of five clubs that together run their own small basketball league. This group, made up of the right people to get the job done, was a great re-Design team. They really knew the settings well, and they recognized both the limitations and possibilities of making change.

The group wanted to increase parity and participation, so they implemented mandatory "line changes" where the whole team is substituted at specific times during the game. They also wanted to promote sportsmanship and a sense of unity, so they implemented a unity circle before the game. During the unity circle, they explain the rules and then players engage in handshakes they have created with the other team.

Memphis Athletic Ministries (MAM)

After attending 2014's SSRD conference, Randy Odom, Russell Jung and Dominique McNear, members of the leadership team at the Memphis Athletic Ministries (MAM), went back to Memphis excited to make changes to their sports programs. In a community like Memphis, where traditional sports dominate the culture, it's rare to find sports programs where the focus is on providing a positive experience for all youth in sport, not only the elite. But the staff at MAM are making participation a priority.

To encourage more participation in their summer programs and to make use of their under-utilized golf course, they incorporated "FootGolf" into their program offerings by changing the course to include holes big enough for soccer balls. The object of FootGolf is to kick the ball around the course and into the holes in as few kicks as possible, just like golf.

Play Rugby USA

Mark Griffin has been a member of the SSRD community from the very beginning. He served as a mentor at two of the SSRD conferences and has made sure that his staff is fully oriented towards the SSRD approach. At each of the conferences, he has shared some of the great tweaks to the game that he has made to make sure that kids feel engaged in the new sport of rugby. After the 2014 conference, he not only inspired others, but was himself inspired by another of our mentors, Lawrence Cann of Street Soccer USA. As Lawrence explained the Green Card, Mark was immediately drawn to the simplicity of rewarding, in a meaningful way, good behavior instead of only penalizing bad. He and his team went about implementing the Green Card at Play Rugby USA that spring.

As our SSRD community of practice continues to grow, we remain committed to staying connected with and learning from the practitioners who go out and re-Design. Like the good re-Designers that we are, we not only tinker with our youth sports environments, but we also tinker with our SSRD methodology and framework. The lessons we learn from the people in the field are invaluable as we think about how to encourage more people to follow their lead.

In order to be even more effective, we hope that our Community of Practice will continue to grow. In particular, we hope that more academics will get involved in studying SSRD and more funders will support practitioners' SSRD efforts. Ideally, we would have an entire army of researchers and trained academics who were ready and motivated to go out and help measure and evaluate the effectiveness of the re-Designs that our innovative practitioners are implementing. If we are truly going to be an outcomes-focused methodology, it will be important for us to know when we are or aren't achieving those outcomes.

If we really want more people to start re-Designing their programs with specific outcomes in mind, we're going to have to get more people in the funding community to support the idea. Any funder who already believes that sport, when implemented intentionally, can have a positive impact on youth should be drawn to the idea of proactively designing sports experiences for particular outcomes. With the help of the SSRD methods, sport programs could show their commitment to an outcomes-based approach and better understand their impact. We believe that funders could be a particularly high-leverage part of the system that can push for SSRD to be implement and adopted.

112 Conclusion

An Outcomes Mindset

At the same time that we are building our SSRD community of practice, we hope that we are also making progress beyond it in promoting an outcomes mindset in the youth sports world. Our SSRD framework does not mandate what outcomes you seek; only that you consider what you want to achieve based on the needs of your beneficiaries and the communities you serve. If you want more excitement in your game, go for it. If you want to reduce injures of a certain type, that's great. If you want to focus on sportspersonship, that is wonderful.

However, based on what we've learned about re-Designs, it might help to consider the following. First, remember that your desired outcome has to be something that the game can actually change. Second, consider starting with an outcome that we know will set you up for positive youth outcomes. We've seen that there are certain outcomes that bring a high probability of positive impact, or as some might say, a bigger bang for the buck. We call these *high impact outcomes* (Bartlett, Bergholz, & McCarthy, 2015). By designing and planning for these outcomes, you are likely to get multiple benefits, not just one. As mentioned in Chapter 3, these outcomes are physical activity, parity of competition, participation and retention, sport skill building and life skills building.

Planning to re-Design for any one of these means that positive things will happen. Some positive outcomes will be more obvious than others, but even subtle changes in attitude and tone can make your sport system a better experience for players and families.

Even the most dedicated SSRD practitioner has to remember the other tools for change that exist. To really get the most impact in the field we must keep improving *coach education*. In many cases, the coach is the key adult figure in the lives of young people and we, therefore, owe them all the knowledge and skills we can equip them with to take on that responsibility. It's also important to remain aware of how you can leverage all the ways that you can implement *curriculum* in your programs or leagues. Well-designed curriculum can continue to support learning and provide powerful experiences in other times outside of the competitive arena.

Therefore, if nothing else, we hope that more people in the youth sports world will begin to look at their sport in a way that puts the outcome of the participants and other beneficiaries first.

A Call to Action

In each of the examples in this book, there is a central figure who is willing to go out and run an SSRD experiment. This is our ultimate and most immediate aspiration: try something to make your sport system more humane, more fun, more educational and to better serve the needs of your participants. It doesn't need to be a big change. Small changes can bring significant positive outcomes.

The main purpose of this book is to support individuals working in their own sport settings on their own unique goals. However, there are larger issues out there in the world of youth sports waiting for innovative solutions. We therefore want to take these final pages to remember some of the larger issues that form the backdrop to our work in sport. These issues include: lack of access, lack of inclusion and gender inequality.

As you think about your own re-Designs, we challenge you to think about these as well. As a field, we can do better, and SSRD can help us make the changes we know are necessary. What small changes that we make to our programs might one day help us address, at a more systemic level, some of the larger issues in youth sports?

The Magic Bus example is a perfect way to think about the ripple effect that small re-Designs can have on an entire sport system and even a community or society. At the beginning, Rahul and his team just wanted more girls to play soccer in one neighborhood in one town in India. At the time, the issue of gender equality in sport was not the issue they were trying to find a solution for. Rahul and his team didn't start off trying to change the country's perception of the ability of girls to play sports.

Instead, Rahul and his team knew that if they could get the girls playing, those girls would benefit from it—that they would be more active, and that they would learn teamwork and communication skills and how to stick with something, even when it's hard. They wanted those girls to have fun. However, once they got the girls playing, and then got more girls playing, and then even more girls playing, they found they were making the case for gender equality at the same time. They had legions of girls who were living proof of the power of the intervention (and boys, families and entire communities who were in support too!). The simple idea of how to get girls involved in playing soccer *here and now*, turned into a larger statement and part of the solution for how to get girls involved *globally*.

If we want to address some of the largest and most important issues in youth sports, we have to think about the small changes that will get us there. In particular, we have to start with the small changes that become a fully integrated part of the game that everyone understands and follows.

That's how we'll make sure that the Commissioner of Major League Baseball no longer has a problem getting youth interested in playing. We saw both USTA and USA Hockey tackle a similar problem by changing the game. And we know that the baseball community is already engaged in thinking about rule changes and other modifications to make the game more exciting.

It's also how we'll make sure that Brian McCormick and other innovative practitioners like him have all the tools they need to keep the negative influences of overzealous coaches and parents from getting in the way of their players' skill development. If his ingenious strategies of 3 on 3 basketball and coaches coaching one hoop aren't enough, maybe he can bring the Green Card to Playmakers basketball.

114 Conclusion

Finally, it's how we'll make sure that John's neighbor and thousands of players, coaches and parents like him walk away from the youth sports world having had a better experience. If every youth sport program opened up their rule book with an eye towards one or more of the high impact outcomes (participation and retention, sport and life skill development, inclusion and physical activity) and challenged conventional wisdom about their sport—just "changed the game"—imagine what could be possible. Think of how many more children might continue to play instead of dropping out. Think of how much more self-esteem and self-efficacy we could instill in these children. And think about how many more kids would be getting potentially more physical activity from their sport experience.

If we re-Design for these outcomes and others, youth sports can finally deliver on all the expectations that we have for it. It can finally be the remarkable vehicle for positive development that we know it can be.

Reference

Bartlett, M., Bergholz, I., & McCarthy, J. (2015). Redesigning sport for greater impact. Invited talk. *2015 RBI Institute*, Orlando, FL, March 8, 2015.

APPENDIX A

Sport System Re-Design: Historical Timelines of Popular Sports

Football

1938—**Roughing the passer**: Deliberate and late shots against the QB are deemed unnecessary roughness and penalized with a loss of 15 yards. Designed to protect the star of the team.[1]

1943—**Helmets are mandatory**: All NFL players are forced to wear helmets. Designed to increase player safety.[2]

1955—**Down by contact**: Play is deemed dead if the player with the ball touches the ground while within the grasp of an opponent. Designed to make the game run more smoothly with frequent change of downs/possessions.[3]

1980—**No punching**: Players are no longer allowed to "punch, club or strike" an opponent. Designed to increase player safety and maintain order (fights were very common).[4]

1994—**QB helmet receiver/speaker**: Introduced so they could get the play directly from a coach with the headset. This shuts off in the last 15 seconds during the 40 seconds between plays to prevent the coach from coaching players in the crucial seconds before the snap, when defensive disguises can be revealed.[5]

1995—**Defenseless players**: New rules designed to expand the concept of a "defenseless" player—now tacklers are barred from battering opponents with their foreheads or face guards, not just with the tops of their helmets. Designed to reduce violent and unexpected collisions.[6]

1999—**Instant replay**: NFL introduces technology to assist referees. Great deal of resistance initially from purists, but now the league is widely regarded as the best-officiated league in America.[7]

2005—**Tackling rule**: Players banned from tackling opponents by grabbing the inside of their shoulder pads. This is a very dangerous tackling technique—it

116   Appendix A

oftentimes can lead to severe lower leg injuries because the ball carrier's legs can get trapped under the tackler's bodyweight.[8]

2010—**Concussions**: NFL changes the "return to play" rules. Previously players were allowed to return to the same game if they lost consciousness. Now if a player loses consciousness or shows signs of a concussion (i.e. headaches, can't remember plays/assignments, dizziness) then he cannot return to the same game.[9]

2011—**Kickoffs**: Kickoff line moved from the 30-yard line to the 35-yard line to increase touchbacks. Very controversial rule because it basically eliminated the art of the kick-off return.[10]

2011—**Boise State rule**: NFL mandates all playing fields must remain green unless permission is granted by the league. Attempt to avoid playing turfs that are painted in different colors like Boise State's blue field (preventative measure to prohibit advertisers from paying millions to paint the field the color of their company's logo.)[11]

2012—**Rules during punts**: Defenders are no longer allowed to jump over the punt shield blockers. This was also in an effort to increase safety and reduce head injuries.[12]

2012—**Helmets**: When a player loses his helmet during a play, he is required to exit the game for the following play. The reason for this rule is safety, to better enforce players buckling up and securing helmets.[13]

2012—**Blocking below the waist**: This type of block is essentially prohibited, with a limited number of exceptions. High hits have previously been the focus of many rule changes, but low hits are just as dangerous.[14]

2013—**Leading with the head**: In the NFL, players that attack other players head-on or lead with their head are now given a 15-yard penalty and possible fine (for the individual player). These types of plays are not only dangerous to the defender, they are just as dangerous for the attacking player.[15]

2014—**Concussion spotter**: The NFL has developed new protocols for addressing the issue of concussions. They now employ athletic trainers to sit in the upper-level booth of the stadium who watch for specific behaviors of players with potential concussions (players who appear out of sync, shaking one's head after a hit, repeatedly readjusting one's helmet, not getting up immediately after a hit). The spotter has video equipment in their booth that they use to tag the play where an injury occurred and alert the team/team doctors on the field.[16]

Men's Basketball

1893—**Backboard**: Introduced to help shooting. Designed to make it easier to score.[17]

1936—**Jump Ball**: The "Designated Jump Ball" era meant that there was a jump ball after every basket. After this rule was eliminated, the defense

Appendix A **117**

automatically receives the ball after a basket. This modification was designed to stop shutouts from happening (up until that point, teams with the tallest centers would occasionally shut the other team out).[18]

1936—**Three seconds**: Three-second rule introduced. Designed to stop big men from camping for long periods of time under the basket.[19]

1954—**Shot clock**: NBA introduces the shot clock, limiting teams to 24 seconds before they have to shoot. Designed to speed up the pace of play.[20]

1957—**Free throw lane**: Increased from 6 to 12 feet. Completely changed the way the game was played under the basket.[21]

1967—**No dunking**: NCAA bans players from dunking. Overtly racist measure was overturned but not until 10 years later.[22]

1967—**3-point line**: ABA introduced the 3-point line in 1967—68, completely changing the game and making it more exciting for fans.[23]

1990—**Bonus**: Starting on the 10th personal foul of the half, teams automatically receive two foul shots for each subsequent foul.[24]

2004—**More offense**: New rules introduced to curb hand checking, clarify blocking and call defensive three seconds. All these modifications were designed to make it easier for offensive players to score.[25]

2010—**No more complaining**: NBA will now enforce automatic technical fouls to players who complain too much about calls. Part of the "Respect the Game" initiative. Interesting because this comes in response to market research that suggests that fans think NBA players complain too much.[26]

2012—**24-second clock**: All 24-second shot clocks will display tenths of seconds instead of seconds. This is designed to eliminate any controversy over last-second shots. By showing tenths of seconds it will be obvious whether a shot was out of the hands before the 24 seconds are up.[27]

2013—**Touch fouls**: In the NCAA, fouls will now be called for keeping a hand or forearm on an opponent, putting two hands on an opponent, continually jabbing an opponent by extending an arm or placing a hand or forearm on the opponent, or using an arm bar to impede the progress of a dribbler. The aim of these rule changes is to "get consistency throughout the country."[28]

2013—**Blocking the path**: In the NCAA, defensive players are no longer allowed to move into the path of an offensive player after they have started their upward motion with the ball when attempting a field goal or pass, whereas they previously had to be in a legal guarding position. The goal of this change is again for consistency and to increase scoring opportunities for the offense.[29]

Hockey

1910—**Three periods**: Game went from being two 30-minute periods to three 20-minute periods.[30]

1917—**Moving goalies**: Goalies permitted to fall to the ice to make saves. Prior to this point they were penalized for doing so.[31]

118 Appendix A

1921—**Passing goalies**: Goalies are allowed to pass the puck as far as their own blue line.[32]

1937—**Icing**: First icing rule introduced to penalize teams for dumping the puck to stop pressure.[33]

1943—**Red line**: The red line and the offside rule are introduced to improve gameplay.[34]

1967—**Goalie penalties**: If a goalie commits a minor/major penalty, someone else from his team who was on the ice at the time of the incident can serve it for him.[35]

1991—**Instant replay**: Technology introduced to help referees determine whether pucks have or have not crossed the goal line.[36]

2004—**Leg pads**: Goalie pads are reduced from 12" to 11" to give shooters a better chance to score.[37]

2005—**Shootouts**: NHL adds shootouts for games that end in a tie after regulation and a 5-minute overtime period. Designed to generate more excitement for the fans.[38]

2011—**Wireless headsets**: NHL referees given wireless headsets to communicate with their partners without having to be two inches from one another. Great innovation that provided more immediate, direct communication at crucial times.[39]

2010—**Head hits**: Automatic minor penalty assessed to any player that targets or hits an opponent's head. Designed to curb all of the concussions that are happening around the league.[40]

2014—**In the spirit of sportsmanship**: If a player embellishes or exaggerates an act in order to draw a penalty, there will be a minor penalty call for both players. The committee that instituted this rule strives in general to eliminate deceitful actions from the game.[41]

Baseball

1845—**Knickerbocker rules**: Baseball is introduced with "Knickerbocker rules" where games are won by reaching 21 aces. Completely different game.[42]

1880—**8 Pitch Walks**: 8 called balls are a walk. Now it's 4.[43]

1887—**High/Low Pitches**: Batters are no longer allowed to tell the pitchers where they want the ball to be thrown.[44]

1908—**Soiling balls**: Pitchers are no longer allowed to tamper with the balls in an effort to make them move unnaturally.[45]

1973—**Designated hitter**: American League introduces the radical concept of a hitter that doesn't have to field.[46]

1994—**Wild Cards:** MLB introduced one wild card playoff team from each league to maximize the competition in the playoffs. Two more teams were added to the playoffs per year. Since this rule, five wild card teams have won the World Series.[47]

2008—**Instant replay**: Technology introduced to help umpires on home run calls.[48]

Appendix A **119**

2009—**Postseason weather**: All postseason games delayed/postponed due to weather will be resumed before the series can continue. This is in response to a 2008 playoff game that ended after five innings and left the losing team feeling that they had only been given half a chance.[49]

2009—**Coin flips**: One-game tie-breakers that are played to determine which team competes in the playoffs will no longer have host teams decided by coin flips. Now the host will be the team that has the better head-to-head record. If that record is also a tie, other performance-based criteria will be used.[50]

2010—**Maple bats**: MLB banned specific types of maple bats from production. Other maple bats have their dimensions strictly monitored. This is in response to several bats breaking, and players getting hit by the dangerous flying shards of wood.[51]

2011—**Revised wild cards**: After the wildly successful first Wild Card rule in 1994, MLB decided to add two more wild card teams per league. In addition, there will be an exciting one-game playoff in each league to decide this extra playoff team.[52]

2014—**Pace of play**: In order to experiment with ways to improve the pace of baseball games without interfering with game play, the MLB tested multiple changes during the Arizona Fall League, including the Batter's Box rule, No-Pitch Intentional Walks, 20-Second rule, 2:05 Inning Break Clock, and Three "Time Out" Limit.[53]

Tennis

1884—**Women at Wimbledon**: Wimbledon championships open to women for the first time.[54]

1896—**Tennis at Olympics**: Tennis included at the Olympics for the first time.[55]

1961—**Jumping allowed**: Up until 1960 players always had to keep one foot on the court at all times. After this rule change, players were allowed to jump in the air and leave the court completely. Designed to introduce more power to serves and open court shots.[56]

1968—**Open era**: Amateurs and professionals allowed to participate in the same "open" tournaments. Designed to improve competition and generate spectator interest.[57]

1979—**Tie-break**: New tie-break format introduced to decide sets standing at 6–6. At 6–6 a 12-point tie-break is introduced with basically the first person to 7 winning.[58]

2005—**Hawk eye**: Technology introduced to contest close calls on boundaries. Designed to help umpires judge faults and unforced errors.[59]

2012—**New youth rules**: New rules to introduce the concept of "tennis for each age group." For kids under 10, court sizes were reduced, and bigger/slower bouncing balls and lighter rackets used. Designed to generate greater interest in the game at the youth level.[60]

120 Appendix A

Golf

1898—**New ball**: First rubber-cored balls are introduced.[61]

1924—**Steel clubs**: Steel shafts for clubs are legalized. Up until this point only wooden clubs were utilized.[62]

1961—**Race bans lifted**: "Caucasian-only" clause is lifted from the PGA. First African-American golfer plays in a PGA tournament the following year.[63]

1977—**Sudden death**: Sudden death playoff format designed for tournaments that end in a tie. Designed to generate more excitement on Sunday.[64]

2010—**Club Grooves**: USPGA announces major rule changes concerning the grooves on certain clubs. The change eliminates sharp edges on the sides of grooves and reduces the volume of current grooves. Change is designed to make it more difficult to spin balls. This makes shots from the rough more difficult and, therefore, rewards players who hit nice shots on the fairway.[65]

2012—**Smoothing sand**: Players are now permitted to smooth sand or soil in a hazard at any time (as long as it does not improve the lie of the ball).[66]

2012—**Wind**: Players will no longer be penalized a stroke if the wind moves the ball after they are in a position of address. Players no longer punished for acts of nature.[67]

Skiing

1924—**New styles**: Cross-country and ski jumping were introduced as new styles at the Olympic games.[68]

1936—**Chair lift**: First cable lift is introduced in Idaho. Designed to make it easier to go up and down each slope multiple times.[69]

1952—**Artificial snow**: Several scientists in Upstate New York worked with water and compressed air to create a snowmaking device. Designed to allow for skiing despite little snowfall.[70]

1964—**Boots**: All-plastic boots created to give skiers more stability and increase their security.[71]

2011—**Giant Slalom**: Federation Nationale de Ski mandates that giant slalom skis must have a minimum sidecut radius of 27 meters (roughly 89 feet) and a minimum length of 185 centimeters. Designed to make the style of racing safer and risk of injury by making turns/cuts less severe.[72]

2011—**Half-pipe**: IOC adds skiing half-pipe as an event at the 2014 Olympics, due in large part to the popularity of the half-pipe in snowboard.[73]

Soccer

1863—**Association rules**: Revised Cambridge Rules make way for the first set of official rules for soccer and for the English FA. These rules covered every single aspect of the game, from pitch sizes to definitions of a foul.[74]

Appendix A **121**

1891—**Penalty kick**: Introduction of penalty kick to award teams that unjustly lost a goal scoring opportunity.[75]

1912—**Goalies**: For the first time goalies aren't allowed to use their hands outside of the penalty area.[76]

1930—**World Cup**: First international tournament introduced to decide the best soccer country in the world. Played every four years.[77]

1970—**Red cards**: Current system of yellow/red cards is first introduced at World Cup. Designed to punish repeat offenders and violent plays.[78]

1988—**Fair play**: Start of the FIFA fair play campaign where teams/countries are rewarded and punished for their disciplinary record. Also attempts to cut down on racism and other forms of intolerance rampant in the game.[79]

1990—**Offsides**: Rule change in favor of the attacker. Now if the offensive player is level with the defender, he is not offside (tie goes to the attacker). Designed to increase goals and excitement.[80]

1992—**Back-pass rule**: If a goalie uses his hands to pick up a pass from one of his teammates, this will result in an indirect free kick. Implemented to prevent time stalling tactics.[81]

1998—**Violent tackles**: Fierce tackles from behind are awarded an automatic red card.[82]

2006—**Microphones and earpieces**: For the very first time, refs were equipped with mics and earpieces at the World Cup. Designed to improve communication between the main ref and his assistants. It also allows the ref to communicate with match officials watching game replays up in the booth.[83]

2010—**Penalty feints**: Players are no longer allowed to stop or feint before taking a penalty. Designed to curb the growing number of penalty takers who try to trick goalies by stopping and dummying.[84]

2014—**Goalkeeper injuries (high school soccer only)**: Previously, goalkeepers did not have to leave the field for injuries. Now, if the goalkeeper suffers an injury he must leave the field. The reason for this change is risk minimization, to ensure the proper evaluation of the injury by a coach or healthcare professional.[85]

2014—**Official jurisdiction (high school soccer only):** The official's jurisdiction and responsibilities begin as soon as they arrive at the field. Previously their jurisdiction began 15 minutes prior to the start of the game, the original intent being to establish a minimum arrival time, not to put a limit on the start of the jurisdiction.[86]

2014—**Goal-line technology**: FIFA approved the use of goal-line technology (GLT) in the World Cup. Officials receive a notification/confirmation on their watches within one second of a play near the goal line. The aim of GLT is to support officials and prevent goal line incidents.[87]

2014—**Time stoppage for concussions**: After a series of head injury incidents in the 2014 World Cup, the UEFA Premier League changed its protocol for handling concussed players. Referees may now stop the game for up to three

122   Appendix A

minutes while a doctor (not a coach) assesses whether a player can continue to play.[88]

2014—**New official ball**: The Brazuca ball was introduced to avoid the aerodynamic problems of the Jabulani ball in 2010.[89]

Crew

1867—**Coxless 4's**: Introduced a new event with no coxswains. Designed to experiment with a new style where boats would be faster and lighter, but might lose out on the strategic advice that coxswains give.[90]

1996—**Lightweight games**: The Olympics in 1996 marked the introduction of lightweight events.[91]

2012—**Quick start**: In the case of extreme weather, the normal starting procedures will be thrown out. When each crew looks ready, the judge will announce "quick start" and they will be off.[92]

Snowboarding

1929—**Invention**: M.J. Burchett designs the first snowboard by taking two pieces of plywood and securing them with clothesline and horse reins.[93]

1965—**Snurfer**: A chemical engineer wants to design a toy for his kids, so he binds two skis together to create a board and calls it the "Snurfer."[94]

1969—**Plates**: Dimitrie Milovich is inspired to create snowboards as we know them today after riding down a hill on a cafeteria plate. Wants to use the same design as the surfboard but have it work as a ski.[95]

1990s—**Slopes**: Most major ski resorts create new slopes for snowboarders.

1997—**X Games**: First X Games with multiple snowboarding events brings the game a huge increase in popularity. Main events include slope style, big air and halfpipe[96]

1998—**Official**: Snowboarding declared an official sport and included in the Winter Olympics for the first time. Events for both men and women include halfpipe, giant slalom, snowboard cross and parallel giant slalom.[97]

2012—**Judges**: FIS and the Olympic committee designate that judges must be able to judge free skiing and snowboarding events. Designed to save money and promote consistency.[98]

Wrestling

1921—**Amateur wrestling**: FILA (International Federation of Associated Wrestling Styles) defines amateur as an athletic discipline while professional wrestling is considered a theatrical spectacle with predetermined outcomes.[99]

1924—**Time limits**: An 11-hour match at the 1912 Olympics pushes officials to impose time restrictions on matches at the 1924 Olympics. Designed to sustain spectator interest and keep wrestlers healthy.[100]

1941—**Scoring**: Pin-down scoring system implemented for the first time. Used to be judge's decision; change presumably designed to eliminate judge bias.[101]

2004—**Women's freestyle**: Sport added to the Beijing Summer Olympics, and women allowed to compete in an international tournament for the first time.[102]

2012—**Stalling**: Athletes who step out-of-bounds not due to sprawling away from an attack will be called for stalling. Designed to curb the number of wrestlers who stall.[103]

Rugby

1968—**Substitutions**: Teams were allowed to substitute up to two players for tactical reasons. Designed to help teams sustain their efforts for the full 80 minutes.[104]

1970—**Cards**: Red and Yellow cards introduced for violent plays/conduct. These cards were designed to promote healthy tackling and punish illegal hits and violent players.[105]

2000—**Sin bin**: After experimental trials, the sin bin is introduced for players receiving cards. Offending players were asked to sit in the sin bin for 10 minutes and have their team play with only 14 men.[106]

2009—**Scrums**: Only the two scrum-halves are now allowed to be within five meters of the scrum. Rule designed to make it easier to get the ball out and start offensive plays.[107]

Surfing

1951—**Wetsuit**: A physicist from UC Berkeley invented the wetsuit to allow surfers to surf even in the worst weather conditions. Arguably the most important innovation in the history of surfing.[108]

1986—**Big waves**: Following decades of surfers exploring the largest surf breaks in Hawai'i, an official competition (the Quiksilver in Memory of Eddie Aikau) is designated for "big waves" and for the first time winners are judged on what they can do on these waves.[109]

1994—**Kite surfing**: In 1994 a Boeing aerodynamicist developed the first kite ski for commercial distribution. Sport evolved after surf fans wanted to combine wakeboarding, windsurfing, surfing, paragliding and gymnastics.[110]

2009—**Junior qualifiers**: ASP International has changed the qualification weight at the junior level. Rule change is very complicated, but the change basically allows more opportunities for young surfers to qualify for the ASP Junior World Championships (increases the talent pool).[111]

2011—**Hangovers**: Surfers will be replaced by alternative surfers if they fail to check in at least five minutes before their respective heats. This rule was designed to punish the elite surfers who fail to respect the time rules. Also, the rule came in response to several key surfers showing up late for an ASP tour because they were too hungover.[112]

124 Appendix A

Lacrosse

1867—**Standardization**: First set of rules designed by the father of modern lacrosse, W. George Beers. Lacrosse is considered the oldest continuously played sport in North America. The game was played to heal the sick, settle disputes between different communities and prepare young men for war.[113]

1930—**Box lacrosse**: An indoor version of the game, Box Lacrosse is introduced in Canada to allow players to play the game in severe weather or when ice rinks were not being used by hockey players.[114]

1937—**Double walled stick**: Robert Pool introduced the double walled lacrosse stick. The sturdier frame made handling the ball much easier.[115]

1970—**Plastic head**: STX patented the first plastic-molded head, easier to maneuver and lighter than the wooden heads and allowed players to restring their sticks with ease and form the pocket to their preference.[116]

1980s—**Mesh laces**: Mesh laces are introduced in men's lacrosse, and leather strings for pockets become obsolete. Mesh is lighter, performs better and is more resilient in inclement weather.[117]

2001—**Shot clock**: Major League Lacrosse institutes a 60-second shot clock to make the game more exciting and fast-paced.[118]

2010—**Lacrosse stick dimensions**: The NCAA changed the dimensions of the lacrosse stick to essentially widen the face of the lacrosse head. Designed to make it easier for player to dislodge the ball. (There had been a trend of lacrosse stick manufacturers making narrower stick heads and therefore making it impossible for defenders to dislodge the ball.[119])

2012—**Logos (High school lacrosse only)**: If a logo is blocking the center line of the field, the ball will automatically go to the visiting team to start the game. Designed to ensure that the center line is clearly marked.[120]

Softball

2001—**Bat review**: All bats used in NCAA softball must meet approved bat requirement standards. Designed to eliminate bats that give hitters unfair advantages. Dimensions are 38 ounces in weight and 34 inches in length.[121]

2010—**Equipment**: Softball Rules Committee mandates all equipment NCAA players wear should be easily available for the public. Designed to ensure a player's performance is more the product of skill than equipment.[122]

2011—**Pitcher's mound**: Texas High School Softball has moved the pitcher's mound back from 40 feet to 43 feet. This gives the batters three more feet to see the pitch and react to it. This rule is the consequence of an uncanny number of shutouts in recent years. Pitchers have been dominant; this rule gives the hitters more of a chance (All 5 UIL State championship games ended with the loser being shutout).[123, 124]

2011—**Bat shaving**: National Federation of High School Associations punishes players for altering bats or for using non-approved bats. Bat alterations are

Appendix A **125**

"shaving, rolling, and artificially warming the barrel of the bat." If this happens, the player and the coach will be ejected, and an investigation will be conducted. The player will also be called "out" automatically. Designed to punish players who seek unfair advantages over opponents.[125]

2011—**Yellow balls**: All game balls must be optic yellow in color. White balls are no longer permissible. Designed to create conformity across all leagues/games.[126]

Women's Basketball

1892—**Women's rules**: Women started playing basketball only a year after men. Women were only allowed to show fingers, necks and heads. Rest of the body had to be covered. Very restrictive rules about fouling; men were worried that women would get hurt if they made contact with one another.[127]

1901—**Official rules**: First set of official rules created by Senda Berenson and Spalding. The court is separated in three different zones with three players from each team in each zone. Players are not allowed to move or dribble between the zones. No talking allowed, and players could only move when the ball was in the air.[128]

1953—**Overtime**: Overtime is instituted to prevent games from ending in a draw. Designed to ensure that there will always be a winner and a loser.[129]

1966—**Dribbling**: Continuous, unlimited dribbling allowed for the first time. Designed to create a more free-flowing game in line with men's basketball.[130]

1968—**Coaching**: Coaching now allowed from the sidelines. Before this, coaches were not allowed to coach or talk strategy with their players. Designed to end the idea that women were incapable of coaching and thinking about strategy.[131]

1971—**5 v 5**: Before 1971, the court was split up into three zones and players were required to stay in their particular section. After 1971, the modern 5 v 5 game was established.[132]

1984—**Different ball**: New ball with smaller dimensions introduced to the women's game. The new ball is one inch less in circumference and two ounces lighter. Suggested by women's basketball officials to make the ball easier to grip and control.[133]

2011—**3-point line**: Women's three point line moves back from 19 feet 9 inches to 20 feet 9 inches. This means that the 3-point line will be the same for both men and women in the NCAA, and therefore courts only need one 3-point line.[134]

2011—**Flagrant fouls**: Officials will now be allowed to review the monitor replay to determine if a foul is a normal foul or if it is flagrant. Designed to punish players for aggressive fouls.[135]

2011—**Charges**: NCAA creates a visible restricted area three feet from the basket. Players are not allowed to take charges inside this zone. Designed to

126 Appendix A

prevent players from standing under the basket and blocking players from scoring.[136]

2013—**10 seconds**: NCAA Women's basketball creates a new rule mandating teams must move the ball past half court within 10 seconds of inbounding. Designed to create a more free-flowing game and increase the tempo of the game.[137]

Notes

1. www.nfl.com/news/story/0ap1000000224872/article/evolution-of-the-rules-from-hashmarksto-crackback-blocks
2. Ibid.
3. Ibid.
4. Ibid.
5. www.nfl.com/news/story/09000d5d809f61c6/article/nfl-installs-new-coach todefense-communications-system
6. www.nfl.com/news/story/0ap1000000224872/article/evolution-of-the-rules-from-hashmarksto-crackback-blocks
7. www.nfl.com/history/chronology/1991–2000
8. www.nfl.com/news/story/0ap1000000224872/article/evolution-of-the-rules-from-hashmarksto-crackback-blocks
9. www.nfl.com/news/story/0ap1000000228345/article/safety-rules-regulations
10. www.nfl.com/news/story/0ap1000000224872/article/evolution-of-the-rules-from-hashmarksto-crackback-blocks and http://espn.go.com/blog/bigten/post/_/id/56504/know-your-2012-rule-changes
11. http://nesn.com/2011/03/nfl-implements-boise-rule-to-ensure-all-field-are-green/
12. Ibid.
13. Ibid.
14. Ibid.
15. www.cbssports.com/nfl/eye-on-football/21918026/tuck-rule-abolished-leading-with-crown-of-helmet-made-illegal
16. www.nytimes.com/2014/11/30/sports/football/nfl-teams-now-operate-under-a-concussion-management-protocol.html
17. www.livestrong.com/article/15973-history-basketball-backboard/
18. www.nytimes.com/2006/03/31/sports/ncaabasketball/31jump.html?page wanted=print
19. www.orangehoops.org/NCAA/NCAA%20Rule%20Changes.htm
20. www.nba.com/analysis/rules_history.html
21. www.orangehoops.org/NCAA/NCAA%20Rule%20Changes.htm
22. Ibid.
23. www.usab.com/youth/news/2011/06/the-history-of-the-3-pointer.aspx
24. www.orangehoops.org/NCAA/NCAA%20Rule%20Changes.htm
25. www.nba.com/analysis/rules_history.html
26. http://content.usatoday.com/communities/gameon/post/2010/09/nba-new-rules-technical-fouls-referees/1#.VUE_8NNViko
27. http://usatoday30.usatoday.com/sports/basketball/nba/story/2011–12–24/New-points-of-emphasis-in-NBA-officiating/52208690/1
28. www.ncaa.com/news/basketball-men/article/2013–11–05/rule-changes-designed-reduce-physical-play-create-offensive
29. Ibid.
30. www.rauzulusstreet.com/hockey/nhlhistory/nhlrules.html

Appendix A **127**

31. Ibid.
32. Ibid.
33. Ibid.
34. Ibid.
35. Ibid.
36. Ibid.
37. www.nhl.com/ice/news.htm?id=680812
38. www.nhl.com/ice/page.htm?id=26395
39. www2.nhl.com/ice/blogpost.htm?id=2408
40. www.nhl.com/ice/news.htm?id=621877
41. www.nhl.com/ice/news.htm?id=730165
42. www.19cbaseball.com/rules.html
43. www.baseball-almanac.com/rulechng.shtml
44. www.19cbaseball.com/field-2.html
45. www.baseball-almanac.com/rulechng.shtml
46. www.history.com/this-day-in-history/american-league-adopts-designated-hitter-rule
47. www.nytimes.com/1994/03/25/sports/baseball-wild-cards-are-approved-for-the-playoffs.html
48. http://m.mlb.com/news/article/3370519/
49. http://m.mlb.com/news/article/3746071/
50. Ibid.
51. http://m.mlb.com/news/article/8643638/
52. http://espn.go.com/mlb/story/_/id/7638357/mlb-expand-playoffs-two-teams-10
53. http://mlb.mlb.com/mlb/pace-of-game/
54. www.wimbledon.com/en_GB/history/index.html
55. www.itftennis.com/olympics/history/history/overview.aspx
56. www.nytimes.com/2011/08/29/sports/tennis/the-genteel-origins-of-tennis-and-the-serve.html?_r=0
57. http://espn.go.com/classic/s/moment001214tennis.html
58. http://tennisfactsforkids.weebly.com/history-of-tennis-timeline.html
59. www.hawkeyeinnovations.co.uk/page/sports-officiating/tennis
60. www.tennisplayandstay.com/tennis10s/rule-changes/the-10-and-under-competition-rule-change.aspx
61. Ibid.
62. www.golf-information.info/history-1922–1944.html
63. www.pga.com/timeline-african-american-achievements-in-golf
64. www.pga.com/pgachampionship/history
65. www.pga.com/node/77953
66. www.randa.org/en/Rules-and-Amateur-Status/New-Rules-2012.aspx
67. Ibid.
68. www.olympic.org/Assets/OSC%20Section/pdf/QR_sports_winter/Sports_Olympiques_ski_ski_de_fond_eng.pdf
69. www.nytimes.com/2014/02/23/magazine/who-made-that-ski-lift.html
70. http://news.bbc.co.uk/onthisday/hi/dates/stories/march/25/newsid_2786000/2786871.stm
71. https://skiinghistory.org/history/timeline-important-ski-history-dates
72. www.skiinghistory.org/history/back-future-gs-skis
73. http://sports.espn.go.com/action/freeskiing/news/story?id=6273652
74. www.fifa.com/classicfootball/history/the-laws/from-1863-to-present.html
75. Ibid.
76. Ibid.
77. www.history.com/this-day-in-history/first-world-cup

128 Appendix A

78. www.fifa.com/development/news/y=2002/m=1/news=ken-aston-the-inventor-yellow-and-red-cards-80623.html
79. www.fifa.com/sustainability/news/y=2012/m=9/news=years-fair-play-1693726.html
80. www.sidelinesoccer.com/history-of-the-offside-rule
81. www.fifa.com/classicfootball/history/the-laws/from-1863-to-present.html
82. Ibid.
83. www.uefa.org/protecting-the-game/refereeing/news/newsid=407991.html
84. www.ussoccer.com/stories/2014/03/17/12/17/penalty-kick-deception
85. www.nfhs.org/articles/2014–15-soccer-rules-changes-include-requirement-for-goalkeepers-to-leave-field-when-apparently-injured/
86. Ibid.
87. http://en.espn.co.uk/football/sport/story/246433.html
88. www.dailymail.co.uk/sport/football/article-2761412/UEFA-directive-allows-officials-stop-games-three-minutes-concussion-head-injuries.html
89. http://news.nationalgeographic.com/news/2014/05/140529-world-cup-soccer-brazuca-physics-jabulani-sports/
90. www.rowinghistory.net/Equipment.htm
91. www.olympic.org/fisa
92. www.usrowing.org/Libraries/Referees/2012RORwebfinal.sflb.ashx
93. www.snowboardinghelp.com/getting-started/the-history-of-snowboarding.php
94. Ibid.
95. Ibid.
96. http://content.time.com/time/nation/article/0,8599,1873166,00.html article
97. www.olympic.org/snowboard-equipment-and-history?tab=history
98. http://xgames.espn.go.com/snowboarding/article/7807238/fis-looks-cut-costs-using-same-judges-2014-olympic-ski-snowboard-events
99. www.newworldencyclopedia.org/entry/Wrestling
100. www.telegraph.co.uk/sport/columnists/jonathan-liew/9464997/London-2012-Olympics-baffled-by-the-Greco-Roman-wrestling-grapple.html
101. www.ncaa.com/news/wrestling/article/2012–02–02/history-fun-facts
102. www.olympic.org/wrestling-freestyle-equipment-and-history?tab=history
103. www.ncaa.com/news/wrestling/article/2011–07–15/adjusting-rules-changes-big-2012
104. www.rugbyfootballhistory.com/laws.htm
105. Ibid.
106. Ibid.
107. http://laws.worldrugby.org/?law=20&language=EN
108. www.theinertia.com/oakley/jack-oneill-introduces-the-wetsuit-revolutionizes-winter-surfing/
109. www.thebigwaveblog.com/big-wave-surfing-history
110. www.inmotionkitesurfing.com/2013/history-of-kiteboarding
111. http://surf.transworld.net/1000082028/news/rule-changes-for-regional-qualifiers-for-asp-world-junior-championships/
112. http://sports.espn.go.com/action/surfing/news/story?id=6799990
113. www.sportsknowhow.com/lacrosse/history/lacrosse-history.shtml
114. www.lacrosse-information.com/box-lacrosse.html
115. http://blog.comlax.com/brief-history-lacrosse-stick/
116. Ibid.
117. Ibid.
118. http://fs.ncaa.org/Docs/NCAANewsArchive/2000/association-wide/shot%2Bclock%2Bin%2Bmen_s%2Blacrosse%2Bset%2Bto%2Bincrease%2Bpace%2Bof%2Battack%2B-%2B7–31–00.html

Appendix A **129**

119. www.sportsunlimitedinc.com/2010-lacrosse-head-specifications.html
120. www.nfhs.org/articles/high-school-boys-lacrosse-rules-changes-create-new-requirements-for-offensive-possession/
121. www.naia.org/fls/27900/1NAIA/resources/sid/Rule%20Books/SBR.pdf?DB_OEM_ID=27900
122. http://fpoaofficials.com/archives/2010/APPROVEDCHANGES2010_2011.pdf
123. www.nhregister.com/general-news/20110404/softball-pitching-circle-moved-back-to-43-feet
124. http://archive.cplstatesman.com/2011/03/17/mound-move-softball-mound-moved-back-from-40-to-43-feet-for-the-2011-season/
125. http://old.nfhs.org/content.aspx?id=5449
126. Ibid.
127. www.wbhof.com/Timeline.html
128. Ibid.
129. Ibid.
130. Ibid.
131. https://womenshoopsblog.wordpress.com/womens-basketball-timeline-since-1891/
132. www.wbhof.com/Timeline.html
133. https://womenshoopsblog.wordpress.com/womens-basketball-timeline-since-1891/
134. www.ncaa.com/news/ncaa/2011-05-26/prop-approves-rules-changes
135. Ibid.
136. Ibid.
137. Ibid.

APPENDIX B

Examples of Invented and Adapted Sports

In this appendix we give you an overview of 13 incredible sports. Some are creative re-Designs of pre-existing sports, adapted for particular individuals or groups. Others are new inventions, perhaps drawing on other sports, but created to achieve new experiences for athletes and players.

Boccia

Boccia is an adapted version of bocce, in which athletes throw, kick or use a ramp to propel a ball onto the court attempting to get their ball closest to the "jack" ball. It was created specifically for athletes with disabilities affecting locomotor function in all four limbs. Cerebral palsy, traumatic brain injury or stroke, spinal cord injury, muscular dystrophy, arthrogryposis, MS and ALS are all examples of impairments that could affect all four limbs.

Boccia is played indoors on a court similar in size to a badminton court. The jack ball is white and is thrown first. One side has six red balls, the other side has six blue balls. Balls are leather containing plastic granules so they don't bounce but will still roll. The primary aim of the game is to get your ball closer to the jack than that of your opponent. The side whose ball is not closest to the jack throws until they get a ball closest or until they run out of balls. Once all the balls have been thrown, one side receives points for every ball they have closer to the jack than their opponents' closest ball.

A classification system for disabilities has been developed, and each classification has its own rules considerations depending on function ability:

- BC1 are players with Cerebral Palsy who are able to use their hands or feet to consistently propel a ball into play. BC1 athletes may have an aide on court to pass them their ball before each shot.

132 Appendix B

FIGURE A.1 Boccia

Credit: Boccia International Sports Federation

- BC2 are players with Cerebral Palsy who are able to use their hands to consistently propel a ball into play and have greater functional ability than a BC1 athlete.
- BC3 are players with Cerebral Palsy or another disability with locomotor dysfunction in all four limbs. These athletes are unable to throw or kick a ball into play and are permitted to use an assistive device such as a ramp to propel the ball into play. They also receive support from an assistant called a "ramper."
- Players classified in BC4 do not have Cerebral Palsy but have another disability with locomotor dysfunction in all four limbs. Disabilities such as Muscular Dystrophy and Tetraplegia will fall under this classification.

One incredible modification in boccia is the ramp. Depending on the athlete's function, there are several types. Its unique adjustability allows for players of different classes of disability to play.

The first international boccia competition was held at the 1984 Paralympic Games in New York. In 1989 the first International Boccia Committee was created, and by 1990 Holland hosted the first Boccia World Championships. The

Appendix B **133**

Cerebral Palsy International Sports and Recreation Association is the governing body for sports for athletes with cerebral palsy. More than 30 countries compete internationally.

For more information about boccia, visit:

- www.bisfed.com
- http://paralympics.org.uk/paralympicsports/boccia

Bossaball

Bossaball is a new sport offering a challenge to talented athletes. Invented in Spain, bossaball includes elements of soccer, gymnastics and capoeira (a form of Brazilian martial arts that combines dance and acrobatics).

The game is played by two teams of three to five players. The goal of the game is to have the volleyball-sized, inflatable ball land on the opponent's side of the court. The court, essentially an inflatable, bouncy volleyball court, is divided into two halves by a net that can be raised and lowered depending on the ability of the athletes. Each side also incorporates a round trampoline centered near the net. Players jump and engage in acrobatic movements that propel them along the court. The rules of play reflect the increased range of movement of the players.

Scoring is tiered depending on where the ball lands and what surface of the body struck it. A player can hit the ball once with their hand, or twice with any other body part. If a player hits the ball with their hand into the opponent's playing area, their team gets 1 point. If they hit it into the opponent's trampoline, they are awarded 3 points. However, if a player uses a body part other than the hand (for example, their foot) and lands the ball into the opponent's playing area they are awarded 3 points. If, while using their foot, they are able to land it in the

FIGURE A.2 Bossaball

Credit: Nyttend / Wikimedia Commons

opponent's trampoline area, they receive 5 points. A maximum of five touches per team is allowed. Defensive play can also happen at the net with players blocking much in the same way volleyball is played. The first team to 25 points wins.

An important part of the game is the Samba Referee. This is the person responsible for making calls during the game. But they also function as a DJ charged with bringing music, drums and microphones that are played throughout the game.

Filip Eyckmans created bossaball in 2003. He was inspired by Brazilian beach volleyball matches and capoeira, and wanted to create a game that combined music, flair and several different elements from popular beach sports.

Currently bossaball is being played in 12 different nations. Bossaball Sports S.L. based in Spain and Music and Sports BV of Holland have united to create an international headquarters for Bossaball International.

For more information about bossaball, visit:

- www.bossaballsports.com
- www.facebook.com/bossaballinternational
- www.whoinventedthe.com/who-invented-bossaball

Broomball

Broomball is a popular recreational sport that is a hybrid mix of ice, roller and street hockey.

Broomball is played in a hockey rink and has the same team and game structure as traditional ice hockey: five players and a goaltender, with the objective of scoring more points than the other team by hitting a small ball into the opposing team's net. Goals are scored by hitting the ball with the broom into the hockey net past the opponent's keeper.

The biggest difference between broomball and hockey is in the equipment. Players wear standard tennis shoes or other athletic rubber-soled shoes, instead of ice skates. Instead of a hockey stick, they hold a broom, which is a wooden or metal shaft with a hard rubber end. Originally, the broom was an actual corn broom that had the bristles covered with tape or cut off. Instead of a puck, teams play with a ball that is similar in diameter to a size 1 soccer ball. Mouth guards and helmets are worn for safety, but helmets need not be regulation hockey. The rink surface itself is prepared in a drier and smoother fashion that for traditional ice hockey, which increases the ability of players to get traction on the ice in their shoes.

FIGURE A.3 Broomball
Credit: Wikimedia Commons

Appendix B **137**

There is no official history of broomball, though most believe that it originated in Canada in the early 1900s and was first played by car workers. From there, it spread south to the United States, first in Minnesota in the 1930s, and today is played in numerous countries around the world, including Sweden, Italy, Switzerland and Australia. Interestingly, broomball has gone through many changes in its 100-year history. Sticks and shoes have evolved significantly. Early broomball matches in the U.S. were played with 10 players per team. That number then dropped to eight and in the 1980s, the number dropped to what it is today. USA broomball also now plays with a "floating blue line," a variation on traditional off sides for ice hockey.

Today, broomball has its own global governing body, the International Federation Broomball Associations (IFBA), located in Canada. The IFBA hosts its world championships every two years, known as the "Challenge Cup." In international sport circles, broomball is now considered an established recreational sport. As of the publication of this book, there is an initiative underway to lobby for broomball to be included in the Winter Olympics. In fact, in Canada, the Canadian Broomball Federation is a full member of the Canadian Olympic Committee.

For more information about broomball, visit:

- www.internationalbroomball.org
- www.broomball.ca
- www.usabroomball.com

FootGolf

FootGolf is a unique blend of golf and soccer. The game shares virtually the same rules as traditional golf, but using a course that is modified to accommodate kicking a soccer ball into the holes.

FootGolf can be played in 9 or 18 holes. The player with the fewest shots at the end of the round wins the game, but instead of using a golf club, players kick the ball with their foot in as few attempts as possible to get their ball into the hole. Players use a standard size 5 soccer ball, and holes have been widened to 50–53 cm (21 inches). Obstacles, similar to golf, are a standard part of the game, and players must read the course to assess the best course of action. Since soccer balls are not able to travel as far as golf balls, distances from the tee to the hole are shorter, so that it is still possible to play par 3 at the shortest holes and par 5 for the longest. Players are expected to wear golf attire; participants wear soccer turf or indoor shoes, instead of golf spikes. Soccer cleats are not allowed.

In 2008, Michael Jansen organized the first 9-hole FootGolf tournament. Professional soccer players from the Netherlands and Belgium were the first competitors. Jansen claims to have been inspired by Willem Korsten, a professional soccer player who played for the Tottenham Hotspur and would challenge teammates to get their balls back to the locker from the field in the shortest amount of kicks possible.

In 2012 the first World Cup for FootGolf was held in Hungary, after which the Federation for International FootGolf was established. Now, the governing body has 28 nations representing the sport. The first European FootGolf Championship was held in 2014. In the United States there are currently over 400 different FootGolf courses under the umbrella of the American FootGolf League (AFGL).

For more information about FootGolf, visit:

- www.edition.cnn.com/2014/04/28/sport/golf/footgolf
- www.fifg.org/about.html
- www.footgolf.hu/en/footgolf-history

FIGURE A.4 FootGolf

Credit: American FootGolf League

Goalball

Goalball is a sport that is specifically designed for blind athletes to compete in a team environment where they attempt to roll or throw into the opponent's goal.

Goalball is made up of two teams of three players each. The game is played in a gymnasium or on a court that measures 18m x 9m, with goals at each end that are 9m wide x 1.3m high. Teams alternate throwing or rolling the ball from one end of the area towards the opponents' goal. Bells located within the ball create noise as it travels, and the ball has eight small holes in it to aid in noise projection. The team that is defending tries to prevent goals by laying out across the front of the goal line and blocking the ball with their bodies as they determine where the ball is headed by the sounds it emits. Games are 24 minutes in length divided into two halves of 12 minutes each. All participants are required to wear eyeshades, which creates an equal playing field for both partially visually impaired and blind athletes.

The court is divided into six even sections of 3m x 9m. In front of both goals there is the orientation area, then the landing zone, and then the middle two sections of the court are considered the neutral zone. To aid in orientation to the court, twine is laid down and covered by tape so that players can feel the court demarcation. This creates a visual for the refs and a tactile point of reference for the participants. Additionally, six hash marks demarcate the orientation area with three marks at the top of this area, one mark at each side, and one mark in

FIGURE A.5 Goalball

Credit: Helene Stjernlöf / Wikimedia Commons

the center of the goal line. Observers of the game are asked to be quiet to allow the athletes to hear the ball on the move.

Hanz Lorenzen and Sepp Reindle invented the sport in 1946 as a means to rehabilitate and increase the level of activity for visually impaired WWII veterans. This also allowed veterans to acquire new skill sets: reflexes, movement without sight, the ability to listen and track a sound, and communication. Originally called Rollerball, the ball was made of tin. In the 1960s, the game gained popularity and evolved, becoming Goalball. The first balls were heavier than they are now, weighing almost 4.5 lbs. and were made of a very thick plastic. Now goalballs weigh approximately 2.76 lbs. and are much more flexible (made of softer rubber) to prevent violent impact.

Since it was introduced to the world in 1976 at the Paralympic Games in Toronto, it has only gained momentum. The World Championships for the Blind added goalball in 1978. Women's goalball was introduced in the Paralympics in 1984. There are goalball matches at all levels of competition from youth to adult, regionally and nationally. And there are international goalball tournaments on five continents globally.

For more information about goalball, visit:

- www.ibsasport.org/sports/goalball
- www.paralympics.org.uk/paralympicsports/goalball

Padel

Padel is a racquet sport that mixes elements from tennis, racquetball and squash. It is played both indoors and outdoors.

Padel is played on a small court by teams of one or two, usually two, players. Teams face off against each other like in tennis and try to hit the ball over the net onto their opponents' side of the court. The court size is 66 feet x 33 feet and is enclosed on all four sides by walls. Balls that bounce off the court and hit the walls are still considered playable, which allows players to sustain longer rallies. Racquets, known as padels, are approximately the same size as racquetball racquets. The racquet frame is fiberglass, and there are no strings like on a tennis racquet. Instead, there are dozens of perforations in the face of the racquet. Depending on player ability, there are three shapes from which to choose: diamond (for advanced players), tear (for intermediate or advanced players) or round (for beginners). A pressurized ball is punctured to reduce internal pressure, essentially limiting some of the bounce of a normal tennis ball.

There are two major rules differences from tennis in padel rules. All service must be underhand, and players are allowed to play balls off of the walls. Also, two opportunities exist for a player to hit the ball, one before the ball reaches the walls and another after the ball bounces off the court and off of the walls.

Enrique Corcuera, from Mexico, invented padel in 1968. It gained popularity in Mexico and quickly spread to European countries through Spain. In the

FIGURE A.6 Padel

Credit: maxriesgo / Shutterstock

'70s and '80s the sport continued to grow, and many South American countries showed great interest in playing. The first World Championship of Padel was held in Brazil in 1992, and every two years 16 countries compete for world rankings.

Currently padel is being played in South America, North America, Europe, the Middle East and Australia. The International Padel Federation governs the sport, and although it is not yet an Olympic sport, there is much support and momentum for it to become one. In Argentina, padel has become a multimillion-dollar industry.

For more information about padel, visit:

- www.wikipedia.org/wiki/Padel_(sport)
- www.facebook.com/video.php?v=10152550809827418
- www.padelusa.org

Pickleball

Pickleball is a sport that fuses parts of tennis, badminton and table tennis (ping pong). It can be played either indoors or outdoors.

The game is played on a court the exact same size as a badminton court (20 x 44 feet), with a net similar to a net in tennis. The ball, similar to a wiffleball with fewer perforations, is served underhand diagonally, like in tennis, across to the other side. The ball must bounce once before being returned off of the service. Only the serving team is able to earn points. The game is won when one side scores 11 points and is leading by at least 2 points. There is a line near the net called the "kitchen" line, which is a non-volley zone. Players can't step into the zone unless the ball is going to bounce (it can be hit on a volley). This prevents slamming the ball. It can be played by either doubles or singles.

The paddle, originally a ping pong paddle, has gone through many evolutions. The originators of the game took to using wood and a jigsaw to pattern out new paddles. In 1984, a Boeing industrial engineer Arlen Paranto invented the first composite paddle. The paddle now includes lightweight composite materials such as fiberglass and graphite. The paddle is smaller than a tennis racket but larger than a ping pong paddle. The net has also been modified over time. The initial change of the height from 60" to 36" happened quickly, but with increasing popularity of the game, the need to have a net that could be

FIGURE A.7 Pickleball

Credit: Roderique / USA Pickleball Association

portable grew. Modern nets are both lightweight and portable and designed specifically for pickleball matches.

Joel Pritchard and Bill Bell started pickleball in 1965. One summer at Pritchard's house, the men found their kids restless and bored, so the two decided to look for some badminton rackets as the property had an old badminton court. Unable to find rackets, they improvised with some ping pong paddles and a perforated plastic ball. They got their families playing that weekend with the net set at 60", but as the weekend wore on and they played around with the concept of the game, they lowered the net to 36" because the ball bounced so well on the asphalt. The very next weekend they recruited another friend, Barney McCallum, to participate in the game. The three men quickly created rules, but kept the idea that it was a game the whole family could enjoy together.

By 1990 pickleball was being played in all 50 states. In 2003, it was included in the Huntsman World Senior Games held each year in St. George, UT. Since 2010 the numbers of places to play pickleball have nearly doubled. While it is predominantly a sport played in the United States, several Canadian provinces have picked it up, as well as India. Its popularity has been spread through community centers, PE classes, YMCA facilities and retirement communities.

For more information about pickleball, visit:

- www.pickleball.com
- www.usapa.org

Quad Rugby

The sport, first coined "Murderball" and also known as wheelchair rugby, is a team sport that was developed in Canada for quadriplegics. Its rules include aspects of four sports: wheelchair basketball, ice hockey, handball and rugby.

Played inside, teams of four compete on a hardwood basketball-sized court where teams try to score a point by getting two wheels of a chair over the goal line using a ball that is like an overinflated volleyball. The court markings include a half court line with a circle and two keys at each end line that measure 8m x 1.75m deep. Games are four 8-minute quarters. Additionally each team has four timeouts, plus one extra for each overtime played. Time restrictions dictate much of the play and if teams don't abide by those restrictions, they turn the ball over. These restrictions include:

- 10 Seconds: Players must dribble or pass.
- 12 Seconds: Ball must be advanced over half-court.
- 10 Seconds: Ball must be inbounded.
- 40 Seconds: Teams must score after the ball is inbounded.
- 10 Seconds: Offensive player cannot be in the key longer.

Only three defenders are allowed in the key at one time, or it's a penalty. During a penalty, players must stay in the penalty box. Generally, players are

FIGURE A.8 Quad Rugby

Credit: Australian Paralympic Committee / Wikimedia Commons

released when the other team scores a goal or when they have served one minute of penalty time. Hitting an opposing player's chair behind the axles (a spin) is a turnover or a penalty.

Changes in wheelchair designs have dramatically influenced the speed and mobility of the game. In early competition (1940s) wheelchair athletes competed from heavy brown wheelchairs called travaux chairs. Folding chairs were first introduced in the 1940s as well, but they were a "one-size-fits-all." Differences in athlete weight and height were not taken into consideration. In the '80s, wheelchair design changed rapidly as participation in wheelchair sports grew. Designers were borrowing ideas from advances in racing cycles—from materials to tube technology. Chairs have become more lightweight, versatile, stable and able to turn with agility. Chairs used in wheelchair rugby are manual and are specifically designed for the game. Typically they are divided into two categories: offensive chairs and defensive chairs. Both chairs have coverings that protect the spokes on the wheels. The offensive chairs, often used by players with more function, include a front bumper and wings to prevent other chairs from hooking it. Defensive chairs have bumpers that are set up to hold other chairs and are typically used by players with less function.

Origins of quad rugby hail from wheelchair basketball. Quadriplegic athletes desired to have a team sport that could be played by someone with reduced arm and hand function. The sport was first played in the United States in 1979 at a demonstration at Southwest State University in Minnesota. In the '80s other countries picked it up, and the first international tournament was held in 1989 between Canada, Great Britain and the US. Finally, in 1990, quad rugby was a sport at the World Wheelchair Games as an exhibition event but gained popularity from the exposure.

Currently there are more than 40 countries that actively participate in wheelchair rugby. The governing body for the sport is the IWRF (International Wheelchair Rugby Federation).

For more information about quad rugby, visit:

- www.usqra.org

Quidditch

Quidditch, inspired by the popular Harry Potter novels, was originally a sport only for the witches and wizards among us. It has been modified so "Muggles" with no magical powers can play.

In the fantasy wizarding world of Harry Potter, two teams fly around a stadium on broomsticks. "Chasers" score 10 points each time they throw a quaffle, a soccer-ball-sized ball, through their opponent's three hoops at each end of the stadium. To keep the other team from scoring, "beaters" smash "bludgers" (hard medium-sized balls) with flat bats at players to knock them off their brooms and interrupt their shot taking. At some point during the game, the Golden Snitch, a small gold flying ball, is unleashed, and the team's "seeker" must chase it down. The winner of the game is usually decided by whoever catches the snitch.

In the magic-free version of the game, players run around on broomsticks as opposed to the traditional flying. Chasers throw volleyball quaffles into one of three hoops in the end zone of the field. Beaters throw dodge balls at the chasers to interrupt their shots. If a chaser is hit by a dodgeball, they are out of play until they go back to their own end zone and touch one of their hoops. The Golden Snitch is not a magically flying ball; instead, it's a human, usually a cross-country runner, wearing yellow and gold with a tennis ball in a sock stuffed into their shorts. The snitch can run anywhere within a designated area to avoid the

FIGURE A.9 Quidditch

Credit: Sergei Bachlakov / Shutterstock

Appendix B **149**

seekers. Catching the snitch results in 30 points for the team, and play is stopped. Whoever has the most points wins.

Quidditch was started in 2005 at Middlebury College by then-freshman Xander Manshel. In October, the first game was held and in November, the first tournament saw seven teams of Middlebury students compete. Word began to spread to other campuses and in 2006, Vassar college revealed plans to start a team. In 2007, the first Quidditch World Cup was held between Middlebury and Vassar. In 2008, the Middlebury team went on a spring break road trip and played against six other colleges. Later that year, the second World Cup had 12 teams compete. The World Cup continued to grow with 21 teams in 2009, 46 teams in 2010 and 96 in 2011. The game continues to grow to this day, with more than 200 university and adult teams, the addition of regional tournaments, and new requirements for teams to qualify for the World Cup.

US Quidditch (USQ), formerly the International Quidditch Association, is the governing body for Quidditch in the United States. They host the Quidditch World Cup, which is open to university, adult and international teams. A new International Quidditch Association has been developed to manage all international quidditch events, including the Global Games.

To learn more about quidditch, visit:

- The Harry Potter novels
- www.usquidditch.org
- http://iqaquidditch.org

Sitting Volleyball

Sitting Volleyball is a sport specifically designed for players with physical impairments including amputations/limb loss, spinal cord injury/wheelchair users and cerebral palsy/brain injury/stroke.

Six players per team compete to games of 25 points (with a 2 point spread). They are played in the best of five sets. Rules of sitting volleyball do not vary much from standing volleyball. Each team has three hits to get the ball over to the other side to try and get the ball to land in the opponent's half. Players are sitting and must maintain contact with the floor with one part of the buttocks when hitting the ball.

Modifications have been implemented to accommodate player disabilities. One of the biggest changes to the game is that the net is lower than in traditional volleyball—1.15m for men and 1.05m for women to give them access to both blocking and spiking the volleyball from a seated position. Additionally, the court size is smaller, measuring 10 x 6 meters. This size ensures that players can still cover ground defensively and find spots to place the ball offensively. Different from volleyball, players are allowed to block directly from the service. Also, any incidental and non-intentional interference with another player under the net is allowable.

One development of note that has been made in sitting volleyball is the use of a chair called the "Striker" which supports players with spinal cord injuries. Triangle Volleyball Club, in collaboration with DSUSA Chapter Bridge II Sports,

FIGURE A.10 Sitting Volleyball

Credit: Pukhov Konstantin / Shutterstock

put forth a proposal to create the chair. In 2012, Duke University's Department of Biomedical Engineering unveiled their creation, and a patent is pending.

The origins of sitting volleyball are not widely known, but it is believed that they originated in the Netherlands in the 1950s for WWII veterans. It made its Olympic debut in the 1980 Paralympic Games in Arnhem, Netherlands. Women's sitting volleyball made its first appearance in the 2004 Paralympic Games in Athens.

Today World ParaVolley is responsible for regulating sitting volleyball and revising and implementing rules changes. Currently 16 countries sponsor men's teams in the World Championships, and 12 countries sponsor women's teams. And over 60 countries worldwide have some sort of sitting volleyball program. At the international level of competition athletes must fit into a physical impairment classification. However, at the non-international level, sitting volleyball's popularity is evident, as many able-bodied participants are participating and playing with disabled participants.

For more information about sitting volleyball, visit:

- www.disabledsportsusa.org/volleyball
- http://assets.ngin.com/attachments/document/0017/4157/Sitting_Volley ball_Webinar_Handouts.pdf
- www.paralympics.org.uk/paralympicsports/sitting-volleyball

Slamball

Slamball is a hybrid of basketball, gymnastics, ice hockey and football played on four trampolines placed in front of a basketball hoop. Inspired by the pace and inspiration of video gaming where athletes know no physical limits, slamball defies gravity and provides hard-hitting action in a full-contact sports environment.

The objective of the game is to outscore your opponent by getting the ball into your opponent's basket. Each team has four players on the court at a time. A ball thrown through the hoop unassisted counts as two points, slam dunks are worth three points. All shots outside the 3-point arc are also counted for three points. Games are played in four five-minute quarters. Positions are divided up within three domains: the "handler" is the primary ball handler and runs the offense, the "gunner" is the main goal scorer whose job it is to attack the basket, and the "stopper" is the defensive player who protects the basket by using his body as a shield.

The court is a synthesis of trampolines and a spring-loaded flooring system that can launch players to incredible heights. It also provides cushioning for the athlete to land on as a safety measure. Additionally, extra padding covers the frame rails on the trampoline system for increased safety to the playing surface.

Mason Gordon created slamball in a small warehouse in Los Angeles. He pieced together a half court from spare parts and experimented with the rules

FIGURE A.11A   Slashers vs Rumble at Universal Citywalk in Los Angeles
Credit: Jim Heath / SlamBall LLC, all rights reserved

FIGURE A.11B "Inches Flying In": LaMonica Garrett flying in for the Mob

Credit: Patrick Ecclesine / SlamBall LLC, all rights reserved

154 Appendix B

of the game with five athletes to test out its structure and basic premise. Engaging the help of physics professors at the California Institute of Technology, he successfully engineered his first court design. He was quickly able to actualize a full-court version after working with his recruited athletes. In 2002 Gordon landed a TV deal with Spike TV executive Albie Hecht and the game gained exposure nationally. Although in subsequent years the sport was dropped from programming, it has remained alive.

Modifications to slamball have mostly focused on the court. From the first half court concept, Gordon sketched out a rough draft with round spring beds, one under each of the nets. The court was subsequently reimagined to incorporate two spring beds, one directly below the basket for the defender and one further out for attackers. Then he added smaller spring beds on the wings, which he quickly scrapped for the current look of slamball, which now has two full-sized wing-spring beds. Additionally, the spring floor was transitioned into "an articulating custom aluminum-extrusion edged panel system" which boasts improved shock-absorption technology.

Slamball, though primarily played in the United States, does have a presence internationally in European, Australian and Asian markets. Additionally, Gordon is promoting the start-up of a grassroots foundation in the US.

For more information about slamball, visit:

- www.slamball.net
- www.sbnation.com/nba/2012/10/4/3453434/slamball-history-future-mason-gordon
- www.facebook.com/officialslamball

Sled Hockey

With essentially the same rules as traditional hockey, sled hockey (known as sledge hockey outside the United States) utilizes different equipment that enables players to sit on a sled and propel themselves using sticks and picks.

Sled Hockey rules only vary from traditional hockey in two aspects, both necessitated by the adaptive equipment. Teeing-charging an opponent using the front radius of the sled and propelling it such that it leaves the ice to check an opponent—is prohibited, and the bench and penalty areas are flush with the ice to facilitate substitution for the players on the sleds. The objective of the game is to put the puck in the opponent's net for a goal. Each team has six players on the ice including the goalkeeper.

The biggest difference between sled and ice hockey is the equipment, specifically the "skates" and the "sticks." Sleds are designed for players to sit in; they have two hockey skate blades, which are attached to a lightweight aluminum bucket. This bucket is supported by a frame, which also supports the legs and feet of the athletes. The sleds also have several types to fit various levels of physical impairment, for instance an optional supportive backrest if a player needs extra support and stability. To propel themselves, the players utilize two short sticks—one end looks like the blade on a traditional ice hockey stick; the other end has metal picks so players can push off the ice for momentum and turning. Players

FIGURE A.12 Sled Hockey
Credit: mgfoto / Shutterstock

156 Appendix B

with limited gripping capacity can also utilize sticks that are secured to their hands. Little has changed about the design of the sled, though the hockey sticks now resemble more traditional sticks, but are regulated to 100 cm in length with pick ends that have six to eight metal teeth for gripping the ice.

Two Swedish wheelchair athletes created sled hockey in Stockholm in 1961 as a means of recreational therapy. They invented the sled in the 1960s with two skate blades attached to a metal frame. Additionally, they engineered hockey sticks from two round poles to which they attached bike handles. The sport gained momentum, and by 1969 Stockholm had a league in which players both with and without physical disabilities competed. The first international sled hockey match occurred that same year between a local club and one from Oslo, Norway. England, Canada, USA, Estonia and Japan all added teams over the next two decades. However, it did not become an official event at the Paralympic Winter Games until 1994.

Sled hockey's popularity has grown over the decades, attracting able-bodied athletes and disabled athletes alike to compete on the ice together. At the 2010 Paralympic Games in Vancouver, Canada mixed-gender teams competed for the first time! The sport is played at all levels recreationally and internationally. There are children's leagues and adult leagues all over the world. Sled hockey in the United States is partnered with USA Hockey.

For more information about sled hockey, visit:

- www.usahockey.com/sledhockey
- www.paralympic.org/ice-sledge-hockey
- www.disabledsportsusa.org/sled-hockey

Ultimate

Ultimate (colloquially called "Ultimate Frisbee" or "Frisbee") is a team sport with a flying disc. Originally developed by high school students in 1967, ultimate in some ways resembles American touch football but has many distinguishing characteristics that make it a unique sport.

Teams can be made up of any number of players, but seven is the official number. Fields can be any size available, though 120 yards by 40 yards is standard. Teams score points by passing the disc to a teammate in the end zone. Players must pivot, not run, when holding the disc. The disc may be thrown in any direction, and a pass is completed if the disc is caught. The thrower only has 10 seconds to release the disc, and the marker (the player defending the thrower) counts out the time. Additionally, no contact is allowed when playing defense. Rules enforcement during the match is the responsibility of the players on the field, and sportsmanship and a sense of ethics defines the "Spirit of the Game" for self-officiating.

In its earliest stages, ultimate, and its precursor Frisbee Football, had rules that were closely aligned with American Football. In the beginning, there were no limits to the number of players per team nor were there any sidelines. Running with the disc, lines of scrimmage and downs series were all part of the original game. The governing body of ultimate encourages revisions, so rules are always changing. A change has been made to the size of the end zone, reducing the size

FIGURE A.13 Ultimate

Credit: splain2me / iStock

158 Appendix B

from 25 yards to 20 yards deep, to allow games to be played on a greater number of fields. Self-officiating is one of the most unique aspects of ultimate. However, the game is facing growing discontent about this as some feel the addition of more stringent rules and referees would add more validity to the sport. Others argue that it would make the game more marketable, and that it would speed up play because disputed calls would be settled more quickly.

Although the flying disc was invented long before the first ultimate game, it too has evolved since ultimate's inception. The Pluto Platter designed in 1955 became the archetype of all flying discs. Wham-O bought the rights to the Pluto Platter and introduced the World Class 80 Mold 165 gram Frisbee, which was much lighter and provided better consistency of throws due to its stability. They made the rim thicker and changed the top to help the disc fly better, especially in windy conditions. Discraft created the Ultrastar Frisbee, which is still being used today.

Created by Joel Silver in 1968, the game was started at Columbia High School in New Jersey. In a parking lot in 1968 the first game was played between the student council and the school newspaper staff. By 1970 the first and second set of rules were already being crafted and adjusted. Interest in the sport spread and within two years, the first college match was played between Rutgers and Princeton. By 1975, ultimate had its first tournament, the National Collegiate Championships, and by 1983 the first World Ultimate Championship took place in Gothenburg, Sweden.

Ultimate is being played at all levels of competition from high school to college and internationally. Matches range from pick-up games to tournaments and league-style competition. Currently, ultimate does not have an international governing body, although the World Flying Disc Federation oversees all flying disc sports. Ultimate has been officially recognized by the USOC but is not currently an Olympic sport. Proponents are also working hard to make ultimate the next NCAA sanctioned sport in the United States. Ultimate is now played in over 80 countries worldwide.

For more information on ultimate, visit:

- www.usaultimate.org
- www.wfdf.org
- www.ultimateevolution.com
- www.thesportjournal.org/article/the-origins-and-development-of-ultimate-frisbee

Wheelchair Basketball

Wheelchair basketball is one of better known and most widely played of the major wheelchair sports, both here and abroad.

The aim of the game is to score more points than the other team by getting the ball through the basket. Wheelchair basketball is similar to able-bodied basketball in many ways, including the following:

- The general basketball rules of contact apply to wheelchair basketball. This means that charging, blocking and other fouls are prohibited. The chair is simply considered another part of the player.
- An offensive player cannot remain for more than three seconds in the free throw lane while the player's team is in possession of the ball.
- A player in possession of the ball must "dribble", which in wheelchair basketball means that they may only push twice in succession with one or both hands in either direction without tapping the ball to the floor again. It is considered a traveling violation if a player takes more than two consecutive pushes.

Because there can be a wide range of varying levels of disability among participants, there is a basic rule of keeping firmly seated in the wheelchair at all times. Players may not touch the floor or tip their chairs in order to gain or

FIGURE A.14 Wheelchair Basketball

Credit: Chanclos / Shutterstock

160 Appendix B

maintain possession of a ball. Additionally, a player cannot use a lower limb to impede the progress of an opponent. Teams are comprised of 5 players with a balance of player disability classification so that there is more parity between players within the competition.

The height of the seat of the wheelchair must not exceed 21″ from the floor. The height of the foot platform or first point of contact must be no more than 4 7/8″ from the floor. Seat cushions are permitted for medical and therapeutic reasons, and a heel strap of 1 1/2″ width (minimum) must be attached to the foot platform bars. Each chair must be equipped with a roll bar or other protective device to ensure against damage to the playing surface. Wheelchairs for basketball are made in two types based on position. Forwards and centers have higher seats to allow these athletes, who are more frequently under the net, to have an advantage to rebound. Guards have lower seats for greater mobility.

The game of wheelchair basketball was first introduced to the world through a rehabilitation program at the Stoke Mandeville Hospital in England. Originally the game was known as wheelchair netball and made its debut at the Stoke Mandeville Games in 1948. But the first wheelchair basketball game is credited to have begun in 1946 in Veterans Administration Hospitals (VA) in California.

The International Wheelchair Basketball Federation is the governing body for the sport. It is also one of the premier sports practiced and played by wheelchair athletes. It is represented in both the Paralympic Games and the Wheelchair Basketball World Championships.

For more information on wheelchair basketball, visit:

- www.nwba.org
- www.iwbf.org
- www.teamusa.org/US-Paralympics/Sports/Wheelchair-Basketball

Wheelchair Fencing

Athletes compete in wheelchairs that are fixed to the floor and are specifically designed to allow fencers to thrust and parry, replicating able-bodied fencing.

Use of all three weapons: epee, foil and sabre, are part of wheelchair fencing. However, women do not compete in the sabre competition at this time. Athletes can dodge and duck from their opponent's attempts to touch them, but they are not allowed to rise up from their wheelchair seats. Points are scored much in the same way as able-bodied fencing. In foil fencing, points are scored with the tip of the blade (which has a spring-loaded tip to measure force of the touch). It must touch somewhere on the opponent's torso. Touches are also counted in epee fencing when the blade tip touches the opponent, but the area of striking includes the entire upper body. Finally, sabre fencing points are scored by slashing and thrusting motions with the blade that touches any part of the upper body including the opponent's head. Pool rounds last for three minutes, and the winner is the fencer who gets five touches first or the most in the three-minute duration. In elimination rounds, the winning fencer must earn 15 points before their opponent.

As the sport developed, the need to replicate the movement of thrusting and parrying became more important, and of course with that, there was a need to keep the wheelchair stable. Fixed devices, which hold the wheelchair in place, were designed to replace the need to have a person manually crouch down and

FIGURE A.15 Wheelchair Fencing

Credit: Rob van Esch / Shutterstock

162 Appendix B

hold the chair steady as athletes dueled. Italy was the leader in creating such holding devices, and they were first used in the 1957 International Stoke Mandeville Games. Currently, wheelchairs are mounted on a frame at 110 degree angles to a central bar. This allows flexibility and "lunge" ability for the fencer. The frame also provides easy adjustment so that the varying lengths of the fencer's arms can be taken into consideration. And it also adjusts for left-handed fencers.

Wheelchairs can be equipped with a bar on the unarmed side (optional). This provides the fencer the ability to both dodge and thrust while holding on for stability. Working in conjunction with the fixed frames that provide some lunging capabilities, the wheelchairs work with the athletes' movements. They are equipped with the option to strap the body into the chair for support and to strap the legs to the chair. (For more information on the evolution of wheelchairs, see Quad Rugby.)

The sport was introduced in 1954 at the International Stoke Mandeville Games (ISMG). A demonstration was given by a paraplegic and his able-bodied instructor, Professor Reynolds. By 1955 sabre fencing was introduced into competition within the Games Program of Events. It debuted in the 1960 Paralympic Games in Rome, Italy. Wheelchair fencing is governed by the International Wheelchair and Amputee Sports Federation. Thirty-eight nations currently represent wheelchair fencing internationally.

For more information about wheelchair fencing, visit:

- www.iwasf.com/iwasf/index.cfm/sports/iwas-wheelchair-fencing/about-our-sport
- www.iwasf.com/iwasf/assets/File/Fencing/Rules/3%20-%20IWF%20Material%20Rules%20Aug%202014.pdf
- www.teamusa.org/US-Paralympics/Features/2014/November/11/16-facts-wheelchair-fencing

APPENDIX C

Matrix of Sport System Re-Designs

Outcomes	SSRD Domain	Sport(s)	Description of the re-Design
Accessibility; Fun; Inclusion	Playing Area	Soccer	StreetFeet: Played in an urban setting, no out-of-bounds. Youth determine point values for various objects in the playing space.
Age inclusion; Gender inclusion; Skill acquisition	Equipment	Pickleball	Use a plastic paddle and wiffleball to slow down the game to increase rallies.
Challenge	Playing Area	Steeplechase	Added obstacles—water, fences, etc. after barriers or hurdles.
Coach autonomy; Participation; Skill acquisition	Rules of the Game	Soccer	A U8 soccer league that allows its coaches the freedom to make changes to the game format each week. Ex. Instead of a 6v6 game with two subs, a coach can split the games and have two games of 4v4 thus involving all the players.
Competition	Rules of the Game	Gymnastics	Scores will be based on beating personal records.
Competition (changed nature of competition)	Rules of the League	Basketball	Beat your own score. Instead of focusing only on winning, teams are measured by whether they scored more points than in the previous game.

(Continued)

164 Appendix C

Outcomes	SSRD Domain	Sport(s)	Description of the re-Design
Competition (reduction in over-competitive-ness); Game flow; Physical activity	Rules of the Game	Soccer	Parents are enlisted to stand on the sidelines to help keep the ball in play.
Competition (reduction in over-competitiveness); Skill acquisition	Rules of the League	Soccer	Players do not have one coach but may be coached by six different coaches in a season.
Conflict resolution	Rules of the League	Basketball, Soccer	Players self-referee. The coaches, who coach both teams at a basket, also act as "mitigator" to handle unresolvable conflicts.
Conflict resolution	Rules of the Game	Soccer	Imposed a one-year full suspension for any player involved in a violent act such as fighting during a game.
Conflict resolution	Rules of the Game	Basketball	Any loose ball that two or more players attempt to retrieve that results in a scramble is immediately called dead by the referee. It is not a foul; however, the team whose player has the ball is awarded an in-bounds pass from the nearest sideline to where the play happened.
Conflict resolution; Greater connectivity (between referee and team)	Roles	Basketball	Referees actually join teams for timeouts. They stand just outside the team huddle and primarily listen. They are listening for player/coach concerns about players on the other team (violence, unsportsmanlike conduct, etc.), and they are available to clarify rules, etc.
Conflict resolution; Safety	Equipment, Rules of the Game	Soccer	In a league with lower-skilled players with emotional dysregulation, the referee has the discretion to blow the whistle to stop play during any physical contact, no matter how accidental. When this happens, the referee checks the "possession arrow" (borrowed from basketball) to determine which team gets the ball. The ball could be inbounded as a throw-in from the middle of the sideline.

Outcomes	SSRD Domain	Sport(s)	Description of the re-Design
Decision making	Rules of the League	Basketball	Coaching without plays. Certain spots on the court are identified and then players know that they must always fill those spots throughout the game.
Decision making; Game flow; Physical activity	Rules of the Game	Soccer	No throw ins. Instead the player puts the ball on the ground and can decide to pass or start to dribble from the touchline.
Decision making; Parity	Rules of the Game	Soccer	Kids determine their own rules for picking teams equally.
Developmental appropriateness; Inclusion	Equipment	Hockey	Plastic inserts allow for adjustable goals using the official goal sizes but easily changing the scoring area.
Game flow; Greater connectivity (between coaches and players); Skill acquisition (for kids at all skill levels)	Rules of the League	Multi	Coaches play on the field with players.
Game flow; Physical activity	Rules of the Game	Lacrosse, Soccer, Ultimate Frisbee	After goal is scored, have play begin immediately for a quick transition, similar to basketball. Don't bring the ball to the middle.
Game flow; Physical activity	Playing Area	Lacrosse	Set up small walls around field to reduce ground balls going very far away.
Game flow; Skill acquisition	Rules of the Game	Soccer	Adding a passing clock (like shot clock) to promote more passing, faster pace.
Game flow; Skill acquisition	Rules of the Game	Hockey	When goalie covers the puck and the whistle is blown, the offensive players must clear the ringette and allow the team with the puck to initiate play.
Gender equality; Inclusion; Role modeling	Roles	Hockey	Must be one female player, one female referee, and one female coach on the ice/team for each game.
Gender inclusion	Rules of the Game	Hockey	Girls and boys are on the same team but each line change or "shift" is same gender, so boys are playing vs. boys and girls vs. girls.

(Continued)

Outcomes	SSRD Domain	Sport(s)	Description of the re-Design
Gender inclusion; Skill acquisition	Playing Area	Racket/Net Sports	Controls play by adding a "kitchen line" (see: Pickleball), players cannot step into this line near the net unless the ball bounces—keeps players from slamming the ball.
Greater connectivity (between coach and players); Increased engagement	Roles	Flag Football	Coaches are quarterbacks on teams (a skilled adult quarterback allows players to make more plays).
Greater connectivity (between coaches and players); Increased engagement (more opportunities for success); Skill acquisition	Roles	Baseball, Softball	Coaches pitch and catch for their team.
Greater connectivity (between coaches and players); Increased engagement; Participation	Rules of the Game	Soccer	Timeouts are allowed.
Greater connectivity (between coaches and players); Participation; Skill acquisition;	Roles	Baseball	Shoot for 1:1 ratio of kids to coaches on the field for K-2nd league.
Inclusion	Playing Area	Basketball	Transition Box allows for players in wheelchairs to play with able-bodied players. Rule requires a pass out to the transition box and then back into play.
Inclusion	Rules of the Game	Gymnastics	Athletes compete in weight classes.
Inclusion	Equipment	Gymnastics	Equipment adjusted to be larger to fit taller girls.
Inclusion	Rules of the Game	Basketball	Unified Partners: when ball is brought up the court, athletes can get a 5-second head start.

Appendix C   **167**

Outcomes	SSRD Domain	Sport(s)	Description of the re-Design
Inclusion; Safety	Equipment, Playing Area	Baseball	Blind baseball uses balls that beep with 3ft high bases that also beep, which are in foul territory.
Inclusion; Safety	Playing Area	Hockey	The "boards" will be removed from the court and replaced with a rubber bumper. These bumpers are 6″ high to keep the puck in play but reduce physicality against the boards.
Inclusion; Skill acquisition	Playing Area	Ice hockey	Cross-Ice hockey helps little players make line changes more quickly by having substitutes on the sideline. The goals are also moved around the ice at each period.
Inclusion; Sportsmanship	Roles	Basketball	Unified Partners: run scrimmages without partners (able-bodied) playing. Partners can verbally coach, but have to keep hands behind their back.
Increased engagement (more game play); Parity	Rules of the League	Basketball, Hockey, Lacrosse, Soccer	Teams can earn a point for winning a half in the league standings (two points for winning the game).
Increased engagement (more opportunities for success); Skill acquisition (for kids at all skill levels)	Rules of the League	Soccer	Instead of playing one 60-minute game, players play in two 40-minute games. If they are blown out in the first game, they get another chance to play instead of going home deflated for a whole week.
Increased engagement; Skill acquisition (more touches)	Rules of the Game	Tennis	Modified match scoring formats to shorten matches and altered competitions for more round robin play.
Parental and community involvement	Rules of the League	Soccer	Moved game day to Saturday to increase parental involvement. Brought healthy food to increase nutrition and book corners for reading groups. Made a day of it—all games played in same block/space.
Parity (avoid lopsided scores)	Rules of the Game	Basketball	Teams may only play half-court defense to allow the ball to come up the court further.

(Continued)

168 Appendix C

Outcomes	SSRD Domain	Sport(s)	Description of the re-Design
Parity (avoid lopsided scores)	Roles, Rules of Game	Multi	Coaches can decide how long the second half of the game lasts.
Parity (avoid lopsided scores)	Rules of the Game	Softball	Mercy rule: Game ends if one team leads 20 runs after three innings, 15 after four innings, or 7 after five innings.
Parity (avoid lopsided scores)	Rules of the Game	Basketball, Hockey, Soccer	Teams compete to win periods (whichever team is ahead at the end of each period gets a point). After a period ends, score resets; game decided by the best of three periods.
Parity (avoid lopsided scores)	Rules of the Game	Multi	5-Point Maximum Differential or "Magic Number": No team may be winning by more than five runs in an inning. When a team scores their fifth run, the "at bat" is over and the half inning is over. This "Magic Number" can also be found in sports such as soccer and lacrosse to avoid lopsided scores.
Parity (avoid lopsided scores)	Roles	Soccer	If a team is losing (whether part of the program or not), a master coach will go to half time conversation and help.
Parity (avoid lopsided scores)	Rules of the League	Rugby	Rugby league runs a round-robin tournament to determine which bracket teams play in for playoffs. Every team, no matter the record, plays for a trophy (spoon, cup, goblet, plate, etc.). Teams play evenly matched opponents.
Parity (evenly matched teams)	Rules of the League	Softball	Draft—"tryouts"—really just a skill assessment: players are given number score 1–5 but with fake numbers around it, (e.g. 8346 = 3.4) to avoid kids figuring out system. Draft is conducted by all captains/coaches, and each team in the league gets to choose a player from the ordered list based on skill.

Appendix C **169**

Outcomes	SSRD Domain	Sport(s)	Description of the re-Design
Parity; Positive relationships	Equipment	Soccer	Players receive a reversible uniform so they can play on any team on any day.
Parity; Safety	Rules of the League	Soccer	The league will organize teams primarily by weight of the athlete and stratified by age where necessary.
Parity; Sportsmanship	Roles	Soccer	Even when playing a non-program team, program staff will help coach them too.
Parity; Sportsmanship	Rules of the Game, Rules of the League	Multi	Unified Sports Program split into two divisions in response to coaches getting upset about rule interpretation—Unified Sports = partners and athletes have same role on team, "Mentoring Division" partners are there to coach, physically prompt, encourage athletes. They may not shoot, block, or steal.
Participation	Equipment	Golf	Holes are 15in across (approximately 4x the regular size).
Participation	Rules of the Game	Golf	Players are allowed one "do-over" or Mulligan each hole. May also throw the ball out of sand traps 1–2 times per game.
Participation	Rules of the Game	Multi	Make sure every player plays at least two minutes before the half.
Participation	Rules of the League	Basketball	In 3v3 tourneys, teams must substitute a player in a specific order every two possessions. This is a forced order no matter when in the game it happens.
Participation	Rules of the League	Baseball	K-2nd grades: All kids on the field, everyone hits. 3rd-5th: 10 players on the field, everyone in line-up.
Participation	Rules of the Game	Baseball	Every player must play at least two innings.
Participation	Rules of the League	Splashball	Seven players with goalie, can add up to 10 players a side, if do not have numbers play half court if necessary (co-educational).

(Continued)

170 Appendix C

Outcomes	SSRD Domain	Sport(s)	Description of the re-Design
Participation	Playing Area	Splashball	Course or pool size can be changed based on available space and age of youth.
Participation	Equipment	Splashball	Smaller ball, goals are smaller as well—can use chairs to create goals rather than official goal structure.
Participation	Equipment	Windsurfing	Seven styles of adaptive windsurfers that use standers, fixed and swivel seats and 1 and 2 sail configurations. A wide range of stability, we can accommodate anyone of any disability on a board with 1, 2 or 3 instructors assisting an athlete.
Participation	Equipment	Rowing, Sculling	Sliding seat setup which works on a single, double or one of our two 4-person extra wide shells for various disabilities.
Participation	Equipment	Cycling	Adapted cycles from 2 to 4 wheels, hand cycles to recumbent tandems.
Participation; Physical activity	Rules of the Game	Splashball	Players can use flotation devices, push off the pool bottom, and hang on the wall if necessary.
Physical activity	Rules of the Game	Lacrosse, Soccer	After a goal is scored, entire team must run to baseline before getting back into position.
Physical activity	Rules of the League	Basketball, Lacrosse, Soccer	Have quarters instead of just halves. Frame the extra breaks as rationale for running harder during the shorter time periods.
Physical activity	Rules of the League	Soccer	As players arrive for a practice or match the first ones there go to the first field and immediately start to play. As each field/group fills up, the next field/group is started.
Physical activity	Roles	Soccer	Coach is timed to make explanations only 30 seconds at a time, and then return to physical activity.

Outcomes	SSRD Domain	Sport(s)	Description of the re-Design
Physical activity; Skill acquisition	Roles	Team Sport	Coach plays at a higher intensity and level during games to bring up youth's intensity and skills. Coach must be a support player creating opportunities rather than scoring herself.
Physical activity; Strategy	Equipment, Rules of the Game	Lacrosse, Soccer	Incorporate "cross-ice-hockey" rules into field based team sports. Multiple goals are places on sidelines and teams must go through middle of the field to score.
Physical activity; Teamwork	Rules of the Game	Lacrosse, Soccer	Incorporate blue line rules from Ice Hockey into other field-based team sports.
Physical activity; Teamwork	Rules of the Game	Baseball, Kickball	When ball is caught, all players must run to the player who caught the ball and do a drill. Batter runs around bases until the drill is complete, when the play continues as normally to get player out. Player can keep running around bases after reaching home, earning a point each time.
Safety	Playing Area, Rules of the Game	Baseball	Safety base for softball and baseball. This is a useful example of something that probably started with special populations and became mainstream for the sport.
Safety	Rules of the Game	Softball	No tag plays to avoid injuries— if ball is caught with fielder on the base before player gets there, ruled out.
Safety	Equipment	Football	Goalposts change from "H" shaped, to the current slingshot look.
Safety	Equipment	Baseball	Throat protector, also used in ice hockey
Safety	Equipment	Soccer	Players wear helmets to reduce concussions.
Safety	Equipment	Soccer	Goal posts are padded to reduce injury or concussions.
Safety	Equipment	Soccer	StreetFeet: Ball is a large tennis ball.

(Continued)

172 Appendix C

Outcomes	SSRD Domain	Sport(s)	Description of the re-Design
Skill acquisition	Rules of the League	Basketball	3 on 3 half-court games. Increases chances to make decisions and touches on the ball.
Skill acquisition	Roles, Rules of the Game	Multi	Refs are allowed to stop play at any time for a "teaching time-out."
Skill acquisition	Roles	Basketball	Refs are allowed to "whisper coach." If a player has the ball and is about to make a mistake, the ref can come up behind and whisper what needs to be done. Helps player relax and makes for less infractions.
Skill acquisition	Playing Area	Multi	Smaller field size or different dimensions to work on specific skills, e.g. longer and skinny soccer field.
Skill acquisition	Playing Area, Rules of the League	Soccer	Small-sided games for younger players.
Skill acquisition	Rules of the Game	Soccer	All kids play goalie throughout the season.
Skill acquisition	Roles	Soccer	Staff members are referees to allow for more teachable moments.
Skill acquisition	Rules of the Game	Basketball	Unified Partners: athletes (differently abled players) have to touch ball X number of times before a shot.
Skill acquisition	Rules of the Game	Basketball	Unified Partners: in practice only athletes can rebound their own shots so athletes learn the skill.
Skill acquisition	Equipment	Tennis	Reduced size and weight of racquets and lowered compression of balls for younger players.
Skill acquisition	Playing Area	Tennis	Reduced height of net and size of court for younger players.
Skill acquisition	Rules of the Game	Basketball	Wheelchair player has a no-go zone (under basket).
Skill acquisition (encourage ball control/ awareness)	Playing Area	Soccer	Removed traditional indoor soccer walls and painted lines on the field.

Outcomes	SSRD Domain	Sport(s)	Description of the re-Design
Skill acquisition (tactical)	Rules of the Game	Hockey	3 on 3 the first period, 4 on 4 the second, 5 on 5 the third.
Sportsmanship	Roles	Multi	Mandated that coaches shake hands at the beginning of the game in front of all of the players to model sportsmanship.
Sportsmanship	Playing Area, Roles	Soccer	Soccer coaches have to coach on the same side of the field and move the benches closer to mid-field so that the kids are closer to each other.
Sportsmanship	Roles	Rugby	Parents of opponent can receive red and yellow cards for unacceptable behavior.
Sportsmanship	Playing Area	Basketball	Put up simple plastic chains and inflatable stands; they discourage the fans from being rowdy and standing up, but instead to sit down.
Youth development	Roles, Rules of the Game	Soccer	Green cards for players who do things that align with mission/ curriculum of the program.
Youth development	Rules of the League	Soccer	Kids cleaning up community counts as points towards standings for the league.
Youth development	Roles	Soccer	Opposing coach awards a player a card for Teamwork, Leadership and Commitment each week.
Youth development; Leadership	Roles	Baseball	Every kid is a captain for two weeks—learn how to be a captain, and how to respond to a captain.

The preceding examples were found in the following programs:

Access Sport America
America SCORES
Buck's Rock Performing and Creative Arts Camp
Doc Wayne Youth Services
Harlem RBI
International Softball Federation
John Smith Sports Center
JP Youth Soccer
Longmeadow Youth Soccer

MASS Youth Soccer
MYSA
National Sport Academy
North Shore Soccer Arena
Play Rugby USA
Playmaker's Basketball League
Project Coach
QuickStart 10 and Under Tennis
Soccer Without Borders
Street Soccer
Triton Youth Soccer
Unified Partners
USA Water Polo Association
Waltham High School P.E. Class
The Youth Foundation
Boston University's Institute for Athletic Coach Education

If your program is using another example of an SSRD, please let us know. We'll add it to the next edition of the Index!

INDEX

achievement by proxy distortion 37
adapted sports 10, 50–3, 61, 90; quad rugby 50; sitting volleyball 51; sled hockey 50; wheelchair 23
American Basketball Association 4
Anderson, Kirk 73, 74

Bandura, Albert 12
baseball 33, 51, 70, 88, 89; *see also* Beep Baseball; Little League baseball; Major League baseball; mercy rule; tee-ball; youth baseball
baseballs: electronic sounds inside 23
basketball: changing the unchangeable 13; defensive team possession of ball after basket 4; 5 vs. 5 6–7; full-court play 19, 65, 154; historical example 3–5; later changes to increase excitement 4–5; shot clocks 4, 23, 25, 56; three point shot rule 4–5, 24–5, 56; 3 vs. 3 7, 8; women's 5
Beep Baseball 53
behavioral economics 49–50, 61, 91
Berry, Sam 4
brain injury 34, 57
breakthrough inventions 58–9, 61
Burton, D. 9, 104

case studies 63–82; allies and adversaries 80; high impact outcomes 81; role and control 80–1; *see also* cross-ice hockey; Magic Bus; Play Rugby USA; Rugby Sevens; Street Soccer USA; United Tennis Association; USA Hockey; World Rugby
Change the Game Sport System re-Design Conference 109–10
changing the unchangeable 13–14
character development 36–8
circuit road race routes 22
coach as pitcher 27
coach education 8, 12, 14, 15, 17, 20, 40–1, 42, 45, 46, 63, 73, 85, 112
coaches: parents 41
coach of the basket 7
collegiate sport 56–7, 61
community of practice 109–11; Boys and Girls Clubs of Boston—Unity Basketball League 110; Memphis Athletic Ministries 110–1; Peabody, MA, youth basketball 110; Play Rugby USA 111
Competitive Engineering 9, 18n1, 21
concussions 15, 16, 23, 34, 57
Conway, Dean 1–3, 4, 5, 7, 17, 26
creativity 4, 8, 51, 90, 91–2, 107
Cross Cultures 27
cross-ice hockey 22, 68–9, 80, 90; equipment 69; playing area 69; rules of the league 69
curriculum 8

Doc Wayne Athletic League 19–20, 110; basketball 19; flag football 19; soccer 20; softball 19

176 Index

domain structure 10, 14–16, 18, 19–29, 93;
    see also equipment; playing space; rules
    of the game; rules of the league
ducks on the pond 3

English Premier League 26
equipment 14, 23; basketball modified
    shot clocks 24; football helmets
    and pads 23; MetroLacrosse 15;
    professional soccer vanishing foam
    23–4; re-designing 94; Street Soccer
    USA 78; tee-ball 23; United Tennis
    Association 75; USA Football 16;
    see also wheelchairs
expectations 35, 36–9, 46; character
    development 36–8; competition brings
    out in us 39; interest and fun 38–9;
    physical benefits 35–6

Fair Play soccer 28
Federation for International FootGolf 138
FIFA 23, 28
first-to-arrive, first-to-play 26–7
5 vs. 5 6–7
flag football 19
"Flying Wedge" 34
football: commissioner 33–4; flag 19;
    Division 1 college football 26; "Flying
    Wedge" 34; helmets and pads 23;
    instant replay 56; kick-off line 25;
    see also National Football League; USA
    Football
Fort Wayne Pistons 4
4-square 91
Futsal 22

Gillham, A. D. 10
goalkeepers 15, 16
goals 7, 8, 9, 12, 13, 14, 17, 33, 35, 40, 42,
    56, 63, 68, 69, 70, 81, 83, 93, 94, 105,
    109, 113; "magic" 66; specific 3, 13;
    three 2; unrealistic 37
Green Cards 76, 77–78, 90, 111, 114
Griffin, Mark 70, 80, 111
Griffiths, Steve 78

Hammermeister, J. 10
high leverage outcomes: life skill
    building 18; parity of competition 17;
    participation and retention 17; physical
    activity 17; sport skill building 17
history of professional and collegiate sport
    56–7

hockey 32–3; parents 69, 80; shinny 33;
    see also Men's US Hockey; USA Hockey
Hula Hoop 32

indoor soccer 22
innovation 4, 22, 32, 51, 59, 90
International Rugby Board 9

Jamaica Plain Youth Soccer 1–3, 17, 26;
    4v4 teams 2; no teams under 10 league
    2; three goals 2
jump ball 4, 25, 56
Jung, Russell 110

kick-off line 25

Liberty Elementary School 46–7
Little League baseball 31, 32, 41

Magic Bus 9, 63–6, 80, 81, 113; play area
    66; roles 66; rules of the game 66; rules
    of the league 66
Major League Baseball 110; commissioner
    31–2, 113; wild card teams 26
Martel, Ken 68, 69, 80
Mathere Youth Sport Association 26
McCormick, Brian 5, 8, 15, 31, 113
McGloughlin, Kevin 68
McGonigal, Jane: *Reality Is Broken* 60
McNear, Dominique 110
Memphis Athletic Ministries 110–1
Men's US Hockey 33
mercy rule 25, 56, 93
MetroLacrosse 11–2, 14; beyond stick skills
    12; coach education 14; curriculum
    14; equipment 15; positive outcomes
    11; rules of the game 15; rules of the
    league 15; self-efficacy 12; sport system
    re-design 15; stick skills 11, 12, 14, 15
Minneapolis Lakers 4

Naismith, James 3–4, 5, 56
National Cup (SSUSA) 76, 77
National Football League 33
NBA 4, 5; game clocks 24; 3-point shot 56;
    24-second shot clock 56; tournaments 26
NCAA: basketball 4; college basketball
    26; Division 1 college football 26;
    softball 25; wrestling 25

Odom, Randy 110
off-the field factors influence league
    standings 26

Index **177**

Off the Wall 57
Ogilvie, B. C. 37
outcomes 3, 5, 9, 10, 12, 15, 16–18, 20,
21, 24, 28–9, 41, 42, 45, 46, 47, 54,
58, 63, 68, 75, 77, 83, 84, 89, 91, 97,
109, 111; assess 99, 100–1; brainstorm
93; character 37; definition 85, 87–9;
high impact 81, 112, 114; measure 102;
mindset 112; negative 40; positive 80,
92, 112, 113; rationale 89

parents 102; baseball 31; as boundaries 28;
as coaches 41; expectations 35, 36–9,
46; hockey 69, 80; overzealous 28,
113–14; soccer 1, 2
Parker, Jack 33
physical benefits 35–6
playground 31, 58, 61, 70; hardtop 46
playing space 14, 22; circuit road race
routes 22; cross-ice hockey 22; indoor
soccer and Futsal 22; re-designing
93–4; snowboard half-pipe 22; United
Tennis Association 75
playing time 7, 88, 89
Play Rugby USA 70–2, 80, 81, 111; playing
area 72; Green Cards 111, 114; rules of
the league 72
professional soccer 23–4; division format 26
professional sport 5, 9, 10, 25, 31, 34, 38,
56–7

quad rugby 23, 50

referee: kid 7; player as 28; teacher 27–8
Rohloff, R. 37
roles 14, 27–8; coach as pitcher 27; and
control 80–1, 106; Magic Bus 66;
player as referee 28; re-designing
96–7; referee/umpire as teacher 27–8;
spectators support opposing team 28;
Street Soccer USA 78
Roosevelt, Teddy 34
Royal Belgian Tennis Federation 73
rugby: conflict resolution 92; 5 vs. 5 70,
72; non-stop play 93; quad 23, 50;
7 vs. 7 70, 72; shot clock 93; tackle 93;
wheelchairs 23
Rugby Sevens 79, 80–1
Rugby USA: Rules of the League 72
rules of the game 14, 24–5; basketball
3-point line 24–5; football kick-off
line 25; Magic Bus 66; mercy rule 25;
MetroLacrosse 15; re-designing 95;

USA Football 15–16; wrestling sudden
victory 25
rules of the league 14, 15, 21, 25–6;
change teams and keep your points
27; first-to-arrive, first-to-play 26–7;
Magic Bus 66; off-the-field factors
influencing league standings 26;
professional soccer's "division" format
26; re-designing 95–6; Rugby USA 72;
Street Soccer USA 78; United Tennis
Association 75; USA Hockey 69; World
Rugby: Rugby Sevens 79

self-efficacy 12, 114
sense of urgency 3
shinny 33
shot clock 4, 24, 25, 56, 93
sitting volleyball 51
sled hockey 50
snowboard half-pipe 22
soccer 2, 29, 31, 56–7, 64; biddy 38;
college 46; equipment re-design 23;
evenly matched games 14; fair play
28; first-to-arrive, first-to-play 26–7;
fixed teams 26; Futsal 22; indoor 22;
kids under 10 3; parents 1, 2; playing
space re-design 22; playing time 26;
professional 23–4, 26; small-sided
games 7; substitutions 20; 3 vs. 3
format 7; *see also* basketball: FIFA;
English Premier League; historical
example; Jamaica Plain Youth Soccer;
Street Soccer USA; Triton Youth
Soccer Association; United States
Soccer Federation
soccer ball 59
SOCCKET 59
softball 23; coach as pitcher 27; fitness 92;
mercy rule 25, 56, 93; playing time 88,
89; safety base 19; suitability test 89
Special Olympics 53, 54
spectators 22; Beep Baseball 53; "better
game" 56; as boundaries 28; support
opposing team 28
Sport System re-Design (SSrD): current
approaches and their limitations 39–42;
definition 11–18; five domains 10,
14–16, 18, 19–29, 93; league level 16;
neighbors have a problem . . . and so do
their kids 34–91; sources of inspiration
45–62; why change the game 31–43
Sport System re-Design toolkit 83–97,
99–108; action 108; allies and

178 Index

adversaries 107; before you start 83–7; brainstorm about outcomes 93; clearly articulate why you want to re-design 85; context 105–6; draft your re-design team 85–6; evaluation 102–5; play games to ignite creativity 91–2; prep your re-design team 86–7; program size and scope 105; re-design considerations 105–7; resources 107; role and control 106; seek ideas from the sources of inspiration for re-design 91; seek inspiration and ideas from actual re-designs 90; spark the imagination of your re-design team 90–3; spend time thinking about other sports 92–3; step 1: define your desired outcomes 87–9; step 2: imagine your re-designs 89–93; step 3: conduct experiments 99–100; step 4: assess outcomes 100–1; step 5: formalize your re-design 101–2

Street Soccer USA 9, 75–8, 81, 88, 111; equipment 78; Green Cards 76, 77–78, 90; roles 78; Rules of the League 78

substitutions 95; dilemma 8; flag football 19; official 20; restrictions 24; soccer 20

systems thinking 47–9, 61, 91, 111

Tag 46, 91

teams: 4 vs. 4 teams for soccer 2; fifty players for basketball 3; no teams under 10 league for soccer 2

tee-ball 3, 23, 27, 38

tennis 23, 57, 81, 92; clubs 80; *see also* Royal Belgian Tennis Federation; United States Tennis Association

three point shot rule 4–5, 24–5, 56

3 vs. 3 7, 8

Triton Youth Soccer Association 28

Twister 32

Unified Sport approach 53, 54

United States Soccer Federation 1

United Tennis Association 73–5; equipment 75; playing space 75; rules of the game 75; rules of the League 75

universal design 53–5, 61

University of Southern California 4

Up2Us 21, 41, 110

USA Football: changing the rules of the game 15–16; coach education 15; curriculum 15; equipment 16; padding 18n3; sport system re-design 15–16

USA Football Rules Committee 18n2

USA Hockey 9, 33, 67–91, 113; allies and adversaries 80; equipment 69; high impact outcomes 81; playing area 69; rules of the league 69

vanishing foam in professional soccer 23–4

video game design 60–1

volleyball 92; sitting 51

wheelchairs 23, 54; quad rugby 50

women's basketball 5

World Cup 23–4

World Rugby Organization 9, 78–81; Rugby Sevens: rules of the league 79

wrestling: sudden victory 25

YMCA 3

Young, John 31–2

youth baseball 3; coach as pitcher 27; urban centers 32

youth basketball 5–8, 31; Boys and Girls Clubs of Boston 110; coaches not prioritizing player's growth 7; coach of the basket 7; equitable playing time 7; 5 vs. 5 7; kid referees 7; 3 vs. 3 7; Peabody, MA 110; referees 7; substitution dilemma 8; Unity Basketball League 110